BRANCHING OUT II

An innovative upper-level text of
ENGLISH
for speakers of other languages

A New International Edition

Robert Lado, Ph.D.

Daniel Carew, Narratives & Dialogues
Victor Budeanu, Revised Edition Co-Ed.
Michael Fields
Leslie Anne Garcia
Ana L. Lado, Ph.D.
Oliver Liang
Melissa Locke
Joan C. Mutz
Veronica Ward

LADO INTERNATIONAL PRESS
2233 Wisconsin Avenue, N.W.
Washington, DC 20007

Illustrations: Juan Miguel de Prado and R.L.

Printed in the United States of America

ISBN 1-879580-56-X

Library of Congress Card Number ....

Published by:
LADO INTERNATIONAL PRESS
2233 Wisconsin Avenue, N.W.
Washington, D.C. 20007

CONTENTS

INTRODUCTION

Branching Out II is an upper-level English text. It expands conversation, reading, writing, vocabulary, and usage. Each unit introduces a new aspect of contemporary living (acting, business, travel, computers, art, medicine, etc.) through the experiences of Bruce Warner who, after succeeding as an actor, feels burned out and rekindles his interest in life by visiting his former college classmates scattered far and wide in a variety of occupations and lifestyles.

The units read like a novel and teach advanced English in an interesting way through the lives of Bruce's friends ten years after graduation. They begin with a short periodical clipping, continue with a narrative of Bruce's visit, and are followed by an informal conversation between Bruce and the friend he is visiting in that city. Several timely discussion topics and a resulting writing assignment provide a focused theme for communicating in English.

After the discussion, an innovative vocabulary exercise requires that the student match the new terms with brief definitions. An alphabetical glossary in the appendix defines the terms.

Each unit reviews usage matters that bedevil advanced students. By means of examples, a conversation, an explanation, vocabulary variations, and practice, the student is helped to understand the problem and gradually overcome it.

Robert Lado, Ph.D.

SYNOPSIS OF STORY IN *BRANCHING OUT 1*

The opening lines of the story in **Branching Out 1** introduce Bruce Warner and his friends, who are celebrating their graduation from Georgetown University. They recall the happy years spent together as students and speculate on their future of which they are slightly apprehensive.

The thread of the story is resumed ten years later when Bruce has attained fame as a soap opera star in Hollywood. Although he has now acquired all the material possessions he wished for, Bruce feels he has reached a state of emptiness which allows for no further development in his life. Dissatisfied with his condition, Bruce resolves to take time off from his career and look up his old friends from Georgetown as a way to relax and relieve his angst.

Preferring slower, more leisurely means of transport like trains, boats and buses, Bruce travels across a great part of the North American continent enjoying the scenery, visiting his former classmates and sharing their expertise, thus gaining insight into a variety of contemporary professions and lifestyles.

It is during the first part of his journey that Bruce becomes aware of the bond of affectionate understanding that has been established between him and his friends over the years, and it is this realization that rekindles a feeling of cheerfulness in the mind of the successful actor who now looks forward to the next planned visit of his travel with even more pleasure.

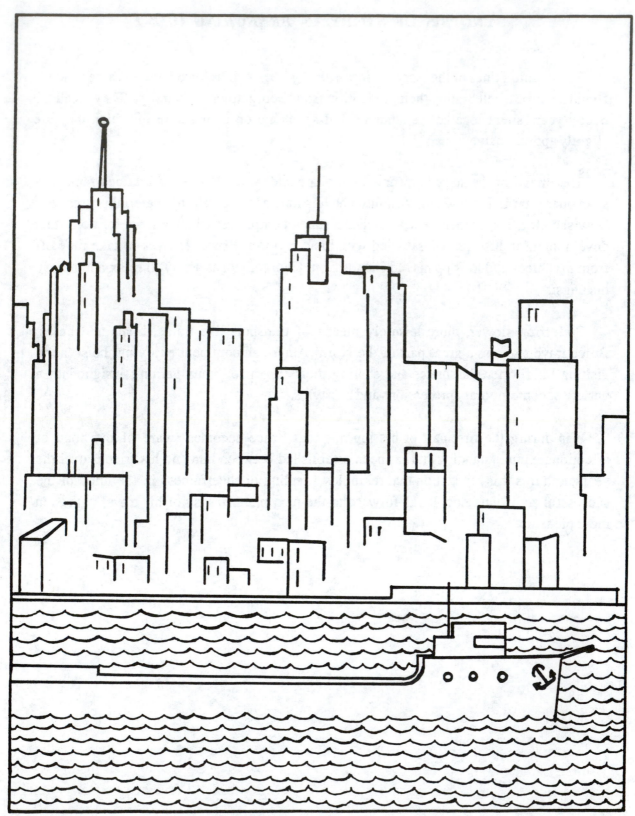

Downtown Detroit from the Detroit River

R L

Unit 1

DETROIT

Atlanta, June 26, 1992

Dear Gail,

Hello! How are you doing? How are Ned and the kids? Hope all is well.

This is just a short note to tell you I'm planning a grand adventure, a long **odyssey** and I'd like to make Detroit one of my stops. What are you up to the first week in September? Don't change any plans that you've already made, but if you're in town, I'd love to see you and your family. Give me a call or write me at my parents' address.

All is well with me. I think I was getting into a bit of a **rut**, however. Acting was becoming very demanding and **dominating** my life. Now, with the **prospect** of this **upcoming** trip, I'm in high spirits. I look forward to the opportunity to catch up with you.

Love,
Bruce

P.S. I'm going to visit your old roommate, Molly, in Boston. Any messages?

Detroit, June 30, 1992

Dear Bruce,

It was great to hear from you last week. I'm really glad to hear that you will be coming out here. The first weekend in September would be a great time to visit. As a matter of fact, we're having a big **Labor Day picnic** which I think you'll really enjoy.

1

I'll even introduce you to some of my **girlfriends** (that is, if your current **love interest** doesn't mind!)!

Ned and the kids are doing well. Billy is going into **second grade** in the fall and Emily will start **Kindergarten**. They're growing up so fast! As for me, I'm still doing some financial **consulting** out of my office at home. But I can only put in about 20 hours each week, what with the kids and all.

I can't wait to hear about your acting career -- maybe your "odyssey" will inspire you.

Let me know exactly when you plan to arrive. We'll talk soon.

Love,
Gail

NARRATIVE

Bruce writes a letter to his old girlfriend, Gail Twitchel, telling her of his plans. Gail responds **warmly,** and invites Bruce to visit.

Bruce and Gail **went out** for two years in college; they **broke up** just before graduation. For a while they had **contemplated** getting married, but they each had separate dreams they wanted to pursue. Bruce wanted to go to New York to act; Gail wanted to get her **M.B.A.** Breaking up was hard to do because they loved each other very much. Gail was the one who **initiated** the break-up. She knew that their marriage wouldn't work. Bruce's **feelings were hurt** and for several years he and Gail did not talk to each other.

Time **heals** all **wounds,** however. After several years, Bruce and Gail **got** back **in touch** with each other. By this time, Gail **was engaged** to Ned and Bruce was **immersed** in his acting career. They have been good friends **ever since.**

Labor Day finds Bruce at the **surburban** Detroit home of Gail and Ned. A big picnic is **in progress** out on the lawn. People are playing **badminton** and **horseshoes,** listening to music, drinking cold **pop** and beer and **making small talk.**

2

(Bruce has gone inside the house to help Gail get the food ready for the picnic.)

Bruce: What can I do to help?

Gail: Oh, thanks, Bruce. Actually I could use **a hand**. Why don't you make the hamburger **patties** while I take the chicken out of the **marinade** and **season it**.

Bruce: When are you going to start **barbecuing**?

Gail: In about fifteen minutes, or as soon as the fire is ready -- I think people are starting to get hungry.

Bruce: It will take me a while to work up an appetite. I've been **devouring** your delicious **deviled eggs**. You sure know how to **throw a** good **party**, Gail. Do you have a Labor Day party every year?

Gail: This is the first year we've had one, but in the past we've had some sort of outdoor party, either on **Memorial Day** or the **Fourth of July**. But I like Labor Day parties; it's like one last **carefree fling** before getting down to school and work in the fall.

Bruce: That's right; you have your **little ones** to get off to school in a few days.

Gail: Yes, and what a production that is -- what with all the new clothes and school supplies to buy. The kids get so excited about seeing their classmates and going to their new classes that they can't sleep for nights.

Bruce: Yeah, I guess I used to feel that way, too, when I was a kid, full of nervous excitement before the first day of primary school.

Gail: So what about you, Bruce, will you ever have kids?

Bruce: What a disarming question, Gail. Here we are making small talk and, out of the blue, you ask me to bare my soul.

Gail: You always said I was good at getting to the heart of the matter.

Bruce: That's right. You know, when I was younger, I always just assumed that I was going to be a father and have several children. And then back when we were going out we used to muse about what our kids might look like, remember?

Gail: Yes.

Bruce: But that's really the last time I seriously contemplated having kids. Since the two of us broke up, I've been married to my career. I really haven't had any long-term relationships with women, and I haven't thought much about having kids. But on this trip I've gotten to visit with a number of very cute kids, children of our Georgetown classmates I've been visiting. I had forgotten how wonderful kids were.

Gail: Yes, I never thought I would make a very good mother, but I was wrong. I love being a mother, and my kids are turning out just fine.

Bruce: You're right about that. They're great -- bright and well-behaved. I thought I might feel uncomfortable being around your children, that it might stir up too many ghosts. But on the contrary, I'm having a blast with them.

4

Gail: I'm glad, Bruce. I'm also happy to have had this time to talk to you alone.

Bruce: Say, do you think you've got enough burgers here? I promised Billy I'd be right out to play frisbee.

Gail: Go ahead. Thanks for your help, Bruce.

DISCUSS

1. Labor Day is a holiday to honor workers. It also marks the end of summer. It is usually celebrated outside with picnics and parades. Name a holiday celebrated in warm weather in your country. Tell why and how it is celebrated.

2. The favorite holidays of children in the U.S. are Christmas and Halloween. From what you know, tell how they are celebrated. What are children's favorite holidays in your country?

3. What if Ned had walked into the kitchen when Bruce and Gail were talking? How do you think he would feel? How do you think he should feel? Does he have anything to worry about?

4. Detroit used to be an industrial city with a healthy economy. It was called "Motown," short for "Motor Town" because it was the automobile manufacturing capital of the world. Today, Detroit is a city in **decay** with a high rate of unemployment, poverty, crime and homelessness. Gail and her family **are insulated** from this because they live in a **ritzy** suburb. In your opinion, what are the causes for Detroit's decline? Who is to blame? How could Detroit be **revitalized**?

5. Thousands upon thousands of babies are born each day around the world. Birth is a common and natural event. Yet for new parents the birth of their particular **offspring** is a **profound** and monumental occasion. From what you have observed, or from personal experience, describe how having a baby changes your **outlook** on life. Does having children make you more **mature**? Should Bruce get married and have children?

5

WRITE

Write a letter of 125 words giving advice to someone who has just broken up with her **boyfriend** or his girlfriend. Include advice on how they might get over it and get on with their life.

ACTIVE VOCABULARY REVIEW

The words are in alphabetical order. The definitions are scrambled in each group. AS A GLOSSARY to understand the lesson, find the word alphabetically and select the definition that fits the context. AS AN EXERCISE, write the correct word next to each definition. To save time, you can do the exercise orally in class and then write it as homework.

1 badminton: _____ 4 _____ to be protected or cut off from
2 to barbecue: _____ 1 game similar to tennis, but played with a feathered cork
3 to be engaged to: _____ 5 man or boy whom a woman or girl is dating
4 to be insulated from: _____ 3 to be about to marry
5 boyfriend: _____ 2 to cook meat over a charcoal fire

to break up: _____ giving advice, for money
carefree: _____ to think about, to deliberate
consulting: _____ without care or worries, untroubled
to contemplate: _____ girlfriend or boyfriend; sweetheart
date [n.]: _____ to end a romantic relationship

to date: _____ fancy boiled egg
decay [n.]: _____ to eat hungrily and quickly
deviled egg: _____ loss of power, beauty, importance, etc.
to devour: _____ to control or rule over
to dominate: _____ to make an appointment with a girlfriend or boyfriend

ever since: _____ to telephone or write to
fling [informal]: _____ Independence Day, U.S. holiday
Fourth of July: _____ a brief time of wild pleasures
to get in touch with: _____ a female friend
girlfriend: _____ since that time

to go out together: _____ game played by throwing "horseshoes" at a pole
to heal: _____ to injure one's pride
horseshoes: _____ to date one person seriously
to hurt one's feelings: _____ to absorb deeply; to engross
to immerse: _____ to make or become healthy again

7

in progress:_____ to be the first to start

to initiate:_____ holiday on the first Monday in September in honor of Labor

kindergarten:_____ going on; happening

Labor Day: _____ children

little ones:_____ school for five-year olds

love interest:_____ a sauce in which raw meat is soaked before cooking

to make small talk:_____ girlfriend, boyfriend

marinade:_____ to talk about unimportant things

mature: _____ Master of Business Administration

M.B.A.:_____ full grown; wise; experienced

Memorial Day:_____ a long series of wanderings and adventures

odyssey:_____ a small pie filled with meat, fish, etc.

offspring:_____ point of view; perspective; frame of mind

outlook:_____ U.S. holiday May 30 to honor servicemen who died in wars

patty: _____ child or children; descendant

picnic:_____ deeply felt; very great

pop: _____ thing expected, probability

profound: _____ Postscript, when something is added to a letter

prospect:_____ soda

P.S. _____ a large meal eaten outdoors

to revitalize:_____ to add spices

ritzy:_____ second year of school, for seven-year-olds

rut: _____ [slang]: rich; elegant; opulent

to season:_____ to restore to a vigorous, active state

second grade:_____ a fixed routine or course of action

suburban: _____ with affection and friendship

upcoming:_____ just outside a city

to use a hand: _____ an injury caused by cutting, stabbing, shooting, etc.

warmly: _____ coming soon

wound: _____ to get help

Gail is preparing for the Labor Day party and talking with her seven-year-old son, Billy.

Billy: Mom, why are we having a party?

Gail: We're having a party because of Labor Day. Since it is a holiday, we're going to take the opportunity to have a picnic, invite our friends and play games.

Billy: Do lots of other people have picnics too?

Gail: Sure. Lots of people have picnics on Labor Day especially, because it's the last national holiday of the summer and soon it'll be fall and most parties will have to be indoors.

Billy: I like picnics the best because we don't have to be as tidy as when we eat indoors.

Gail: I know. You get to sit on the grass and eat hamburgers and hotdogs, don't you?

Billy: Yep, and we don't have to clean up afterwards either.

Gail: Oh, yes, we do. We always have to throw away all our trash to keep our lawn pretty, and on account of the bugs. You don't want to attract wasps and ants, do you?

Billy: No. I remember when Tommy was stung by a wasp. He cried for a long time.

Gail: I remember it too, but that wasp sting was caused by his own inquisitiveness. He should not have interfered with that wasp's nest.

Billy: Yeah. That's one bad part about picnics: the wasps want to come too.

CLAUSES OF CAUSE AND THE USE OF SUBORDINATING CONJUNCTIONS

We're having a picnic <u>because of</u> Labor Day.

I like picnics the best <u>because</u> we don't have to be as tidy as when we eat inside.

We always throw away all our trash <u>on account of</u> the bugs.

REVIEW

Cause clauses answer the question "Why?". The cause clause may be introduced by <u>because</u>, <u>as</u>, <u>since</u>, <u>for</u>:

Bruce had a good time <u>because</u> Gail and her family were warm to him.

It is possible to use <u>since</u>, <u>as</u>, or <u>for</u> for because:

Bruce had a good time <u>since</u> Gail and her family were warm to him.

The cause clause may come before the main clause:

<u>As</u> Gail and her family were warm to Bruce, he had a good time.

The pronoun is used in the second clause to avoid repetition of the proper noun. <u>For</u> cannot be used when the cause clause precedes the main clause.

Because of, on account of, due to, caused by, owing to, are followed by nouns or noun phrases. They are used with an object and at times a possessive adjective. The object may be a gerund preceded by a possessive adjective:

Gail and Ned are throwing a party because of the holiday.
Bruce was a little nervous about seeing Gail on account of their old relationship.

Because of, on account of, due to, caused by and owing to may also be followed by complete clauses with the addition of the fact that:

Billy asked a lot of questions because of his age.
Billy asked a lot of questions because of the fact that he was young.

The relocation was due to rain.
The relocation was due to the fact that it had rained.

The picnic failed owing to poor attendance.
The picnic failed owing to the fact that few people showed up.

VOCABULARY VARIATIONS

Gail and her family were [warm to Bruce.
                    [hospitable to Bruce.
                    [friendly to Bruce.

Poor attendance = Few people showed up.
                         Few people turned up.
                         Few people came.

That's one bad part about picnics.
That's one bad aspect of picnics.
That's one negative side to picnics.

PRACTICE

A.   Fill in the appropriate words. There may be more than one correct choice. Choose from: because, on account of, owing to, caused by and because of.

11

1. The picnic was postponed _____ the bad weather.

2. Detroit is in decay _____ the decline in the auto industry.

3. Billy asks a lot of questions _____ his age.

4. Bruce and Gail's break-up was _____ a difference in goals.

5. Gail likes Labor Day parties _____ they are like one last fling of summer.

6. He decided to become an architect _____ he loved mathematics and drawing.

7. The economy of the country was declining rapidly _____ the war.

8. He was given a light sentence _____ there were no casualties in the accident.

9. He sold his car at a low price _____ the fact that it kept breaking down.

10. They have canceled the trip _____ the bad weather.

B.   Complete the following sentences. Pay attention to the conjunction provided.

1. Many people are unhappy at work on account of _____
   _____

2. Bruce went to visit Gail because _____
   _____

3. A picnic is fun because of _____
   _____

4. One should write a letter before visiting a friend since _____
   _____

12

5. Travel is much easier these days due to the fact that _____
_____

6. Everything is more expensive nowadays because of _____
_____

7. Why don't they turn down the radio since _____
_____

8. Many T.V. viewers are not watching that program on account of _____
_____

9. We had to climb the stairs owing to the fact that _____
_____

10. We never lend them money because _____
_____

C.   Respond to the following questions with full sentences.

1. Why is it sometimes difficult to talk with small children?

2. Why would Bruce want to catch up on Gail's life?

3. Why do people break up even of they love each other?

4. Will you have a picnic this weekend? Why or why not?

5. Do you enjoy parties? Why of why not?

6. Why do they have to work such long hours?

7. Why did John and Mary postpone their wedding?

8. Why did he get punished so severely?

9. Why does a driver have to slow down when it is snowing?

10. Why did you leave the party so early?

The Chicago Art Institute

16

Unit 2

CHICAGO

THE ART INSTITUTE OF CHICAGO

Discover forty centuries of human creativity at The Art Institute of Chicago, one of the world's leading museums.

From ancient Chinese **bronzes** to the latest work by today's artists, from Rembrandt paintings to African wood **carvings**, the **collections** include some of the finest art ever produced. On display are paintings, **sculpture**, **prints** and **drawings**, photographs, Oriental art, art of Africa, Oceania, and the Americas, **textiles**, decorative arts, and architectural fragments and drawings.

See the Institute's renowned paintings dating from the fourteenth century to the present. Don't miss Georges Seurat's masterpiece Sunday Afternoon on the Island of La Grande Jatte, John Singer Sargent's elegant portrait of Mrs. George Swinton, and Grant Wood's celebrated American Gothic. Especially **noteworthy** is the internationally acclaimed collection of **impressionist** and Post-impressionist pictures, with many outstanding examples by Monet, Renoir, Degas, van Gogh, and other painters of the period.

Additional **highlights** include a distinguished collection of prints and drawings, an impressive assemblage of Japanese prints, and the historic Trading Room designed by Adler and Sullivan, reconstructed from the original Chicago Stock Exchange Building. Reopening in April 1989, the fascinating Thorne Rooms reproduce sixty-eight European and American rooms in miniature, tracing the history of **interior design**.

Explore the world of art through free public programs conducted by the Department of Museum Education. Half-hour **gallery** walks or slide lectures on a variety of topics are scheduled weekdays at 12:15 p.m. Collection highlight tours, presented every day at 2:00 p.m., survey the Institute's world-famous collections.

Tuesday lectures at 6:00 p.m. feature noted guest scholars on museum staff. Gallery walks for children are presented Saturdays at 1:00 p.m. from October through June. For recorded program information, call 443-3500.

NARRATIVE

Bruce visits his friend Hannah Cohn in Chicago. Hannah is a "starving artist." She does **freelance** work as a **commercial graphic artist** to make money. Her real love and **vocation**, however, is painting. Hannah has a studio on Chicago's North Side. Today, Hannah takes Bruce on a tour of her Chicago. She shows him her **canvases** at the studio. Then they have coffee at an **artsy** cafe on the North Side. They take the "L," Chicago's **mass transit system**, to the Art Institute. Hannah proves to be an excellent guide to the Museum's collections. Bruce learns many new things about art. They continue their conversation out on the sidewalk. The **hustle and bustle** of this grey Chicago afternoon fail to disturb them because they are so **engrossed** in conversation. Thus engaged, they wander around Chicago's downtown -- the Loop.

DIALOGUE

Bruce: My **preference** has always been for more **realistic** art. I don't like abstract painting.

Hannah: Oh Bruce, don't be a **philistine**! **Abstract art** is wonderful. If you want a realistic representation then take a **snapshot**. Paintings can teach you to look at the world in a whole new way. Some abstract paintings are simply **sublime**.

18

Bruce: But some of those paintings we saw a child could have painted. Even I could have painted them! And I don't know one end of a **paint brush** from another.

Hannah: Bruce, Bruce, Bruce. What did you think of those Picasso's we saw?

Bruce: Well his earlier works I like because they look like things in the real world. The later paintings are just **blobs** of color.

Hannah: That's not true at all. Do you know that painting of Picasso's of a woman descending the stairs?

Bruce: Yes.

Hannah: By using simple geometric shapes, Picasso conveys a sense of motion. It almost seems as if the woman in the painting is moving.

Bruce: You have a point there. In fact, there is a kind of painting which is not very realistic which I like very much -- Impressionist painting.

Hannah: You see. The French Impressionists are loved all over the world for their work. They paint an **impression** of a flower, a person or a **pastoral** setting, for example. They use points, blobs and **smudges** of color to paint a mountain or a cathedral. Some of their paintings even seem to give off light.

Bruce: Well, you've **convinced** me to be more **open-minded** about art. Going to a museum with an artist is a good way to learn about art.

Hannah: Although I've been to the museum a million times, each time I go I get new ideas for my work.

Bruce: All of this talk has made me hungry.

Hannah: My **grant** just came through, so let me buy you lunch at Burger King.

DISCUSS

1.	Which is better, realistic or abstract art?

2.	Artists used to survive by having a **patron**. How can artists get funding today? Should society pay artists? Would there be more arts if there were more public funding of art? If an artist is "Starving," is he or she more creative?

3.	How is Asian art different from Western art?

4.	Artists from different countries borrow from each other. Is this kind of mixing a good thing? Is it better to preserve past styles or to create new ones?

5.	In Washington D.C., during 1989, an art show was canceled because some people thought the art was obscene. Should art be censored or restricted?

WRITE

Art has been called an international language. Can art help promote international peace. If so, how? Write your thoughts in a 125-word essay.

ACTIVE VOCABULARY REVIEW

The words are in alphabetical order. The definitions are scrambled in each group. AS A GLOSSARY to understand the lesson, find the word alphabetically and select the definition that fits the context. AS AN EXERCISE, write the correct word next to each definition. To save time, you can do the exercise orally in class and then write it as homework.

abstract art: _____ beautiful handwriting

artsy [informal]: _____ a sculpture made of bronze metal

blob: _____ art which represents symbols and not realities

bronze: _____ a small drop (of color)

calligraphy: _____ trying to be artistic

canvas: _____ of or pertaining to business

carving: _____ the make-up or arrangement of a thing

collection: _____ a sculpture made of wood

commercial: _____ group of items gathered from various places

composition: _____ an oil painting (on canvas)

to convince: _____ food one eats at McDonald's, Burger King, etc.

drawing: _____ to persuade by argument or evidence

to engross: _____ a writer or artist who takes on special jobs

fast food: _____ to take the entire attention of

freelancer: _____ an art piece made with pencil or pen

gallery: _____ busy, noisy activity

grant: _____ draws, designs, diagrams for commercial purposes

graphic artist: _____ money given to create art or do research

highlight: _____ a place where art is displayed

hustle and bustle: _____ the most important or interesting part

image: _____ decorating the inside of homes, offices, etc.

Impressionists: _____ subways and buses in cities

interior design: _____ a representation of a person or thing

landscape: _____ Monet, Picasso, Degas, Seurat, Van Gogh, etc.

mass transit system: _____ painting of an outdoor view

noteworthy: _____ impartial; realistic

objective: _____ used to paint pictures

oil painting: _____ important; significant; remarkable

open-minded: _____ picture in colors with an oil base

paint brush: _____ willing to consider new ideas

pastoral: _____ a picture of a person

patron: _____ of country life

philistine: _____ person who financially supports an artist

pop art: _____ narrow-minded person without culture

portrait: _____ depicts objects of popular culture

preference: _____ accurately representing the real world

print: _____ a work of art carved or modeled from wood, stone, metal, etc.

realistic: _____ attitude of liking better

scroll: _____ printed copy of a work of art

sculpture: _____ a painting which can be rolled up

smudge: _____ sculpture of a human being or animal

snapshot: _____ painting of inanimate objects, e.g. fruit, flowers, etc.

starving artist: _____ a dirty spot; a smear

statue: _____ artist without much money

still life: _____ photograph taken in an instant

subjective: _____ painting done with water-based paint

sublime: _____ a woven fabric or cloth

textile: _____ feeling that one is called to a career

vocation: _____ biased; partial; nonobjective

watercolor: _____ inspiring awe; majestic

John: Hi, Lisa. Are you going to the library after class?

Lisa: Yes. I've got a test next week in my most difficult class.

John: Oh? What is it?

Lisa: It's a pretty advanced class in animal physiology, and the professor demands excellent work.

John: Do you do experiments on a lot of dead animals?

Lisa: Sometimes we do, but we also spend a lot of time looking at microscopic organisms which would be quite invisible to the naked eye.

John: That sounds very interesting. Well, I'd better let you go on to the library to study then. I know you want to write a perfect exam.

Lisa: Okay. Bye John.

John: Bye Lisa.

GRADABLE Adjectives:

My most <u>difficult</u> class.
That sounds very <u>interesting</u>.

Non-GRADABLE Adjectives:

The professor demanded <u>excellent</u> work.
Do you do experiments on a lot of <u>dead</u> animals?
You want to write a <u>perfect</u> exam.
Those organisms would be quite <u>invisible</u> to the naked eye.

REVIEW

Adjectives can be divided into two groups: GRADABLE and NON-GRADABLE.
Most adjectives are gradable.

Gradable adjectives
1. Can be used in the comparative or superlative forms.
    e.g. shorter, the most expensive

2. Can be modified by adverbs of degree or intensity.
    e.g. rather short; very expensive

Non-gradable adjectives
1. Cannot be used in the comparative or superlative forms.
    For example, you **cannot** say: more wonderful; the most invisible.

2. Cannot be logically modified by adverbs of degree or intensity.
    If this is done, the result is either redundant or unintelligible.
    For example, you **cannot** say: extremely wonderful; very invisible.

Following are some common adverbs of degree and intensity: A bit, a little, quite,
rather, somewhat, too, very, absolutely, completely, extremely, totally. They cannot
be used with non-gradable adjectives in certain situations.

Following are some common non-gradable adjectives: alive, daily, dead, different, empty, enormous, first, horrible, impossible, infinite, irresistible, mental, perfect, pregnant, right, wonderful, wrong, unique.

Exceptions:
- When quite is used with a non-gradable adjective it means "completely"
  e.g. quite dead, or "more than expected" e.g. quite enormous.

- When rather is used with a non-gradable adjective it means "surprisingly"
  e.g. rather unique.

- Non-gradable adjectives can be modified by determiners of quantity, e.g. One
  right response; Many perfect students.

VOCABULARY VARIATIONS

Compare and contrast the following:

The professor demanded excellent work.
The professor only accepted work of a high caliber.
The professor required quality work.

Well, I'd better let you go on to the library.
Well, I won't keep you from studying any longer.
Well, I'll leave you now, so you can go on to the library.

I know you want to write a perfect exam.
I know you want to do well on the exam.
I know you want to pass your exam with flying colors.

A. Fill in the blanks with a modifier of your choice or leave a space as you see fit. Use the following list : *many, so, quite, very, rather, completely, a little.* The modifier can be used several times if necessary.

Images of certain **landscapes** are _____ irresistible to me. I am sometimes moved to try to capture them in paintings or photographs. I have _____ beautiful pictures of the Southwestern region of the United States. The desert and sky seem _____ alive with color, and every sunset is _____ unique. Since the Grand Canyon is _____ enormous, it can look _____ different in different places. Even though it could be _____ dangerous, I think a trip into the Grand Canyon would be a _____ perfect vacation for an artist.

B. Are the following phrases incorrect because they are *redundant* or *unintelligible?*
   e.g. Very perfect > redundant!

1. Rather alive
2. Very daily
3. Extremely invisible
4. Too dead
5. Endlessly infinite
6. Somewhat pregnant
7. More inferior
8. Too unique
9. Very excellent
10. Neatly superior

C. Think of or find a gradable adjective with a modifier that would match the non-gradable adjective provided.

Gradable e.g. very bad	Non-gradable horrendous
1.	excellent
2.	exhausted
3.	hypersensitive
4.	gigantic
5.	frozen
6.	superior
7.	principal
8.	perfect
9.	plural
10.	manifold

Madison: Modern Medicine

28

Unit 3

MADISON

The Recycled Man

CONSIDER THIS scenario: Dan Smith is injured in a boating accident. **Physicians** certify that his brain has quit functioning. Although medical equipment can maintain his **heartbeat**, he is dead. A nurse enters his **Social Security number** into a computer and the screen flashes "Universal **Donor**." The display notes that Dan's wife had approved his decision (and **signed up** herself).

The hospital calls the local **organ** and **tissue** center, and late that evening doctors remove Dan's pancreas, liver, kidneys, lungs and heart. They also take more than 70 kinds of tissue -- **corneas**, skin, bones, **ligaments** and **tendons**, **veins** and **middle ears** -- with procedures so careful that the family can still have an open-**casket funeral** the next day.

Within 24 hours, elements of Dan's body are used to release two kidney patients from the **rigors** of **dialysis**. His heart saves a 40-year-old father of two. His lungs give life to a steelworker and a grandmother. His liver saves a college student, and his pancreas is **transplanted** to a young **diabetic**.

In the next few days, he gives hearing to one child and eyesight to two others. His skin helps two burned firefighters. Other tissues aid in reconstructive surgery. Some of his bones are freeze-dried for **dental** and other use; some tissues are assigned to research labs.

Computer networks help **allocate** the material, allowing physicians to find a proper **match** (hip and knee bones, for example, are cut to fit specific patients) and all transplant results are fed into a **data bank** shared by **clinicians** and researchers.

The **collective** value of these procedures runs to millions of dollars. The lives saved and suffering relieved are **priceless**. Yet the cost of Dan's tissues and organs is zero. All were **donated**. This is no **futuristic daydream**. Each of the medical techniques and communication technologies described above exists today.

-- Joel L. Swerdlow

29

NARRATIVE

From Chicago, Bruce takes a bus ride north to Madison, Wisconsin. He passes cornfields and **dairies**, **rolling** hills and small towns. After three hours, he pulls in to Madison. School is just starting up at the University of Wisconsin, one of the nation's largest research universities. Students, back from summer break, are everywhere on this sunny afternoon: **greeting** one another with warm embraces, riding bikes, **running errands**.

Bruce is in town to meet his friend, Dr. Catherine Rice. Cathy is an old chum of Bruce's from college. She went to med school in California and then went on to get her doctorate here in Madison. She is an up-and-coming research scientist in the field of ophthalmology. She has done pioneering work on cornea transplants and the study of lens membrane permeability.

Bruce and Cathy have a beer together on the patio of the Memorial Union, UW's student union, overlooking Lake Mendota.

DIALOGUE

Bruce: As I was walking across the campus to meet you here, Cathy, it **struck me** how young the students look.

Cathy: Well, remember Bruce, it's been ten years since you were in college. Many of the **freshmen** are only 17 -- still wet behind the ears.

Bruce: So, how does it feel for you to be finally out of school?

Cathy: It's a relief to have my **Ph.D.** now; if you only have an **M.D.**, people tend **to look down on** you as a clinician. You're considered a **generalist** who doesn't have much **specialized** knowledge and who is unfamiliar with **cutting-edge** research.

Bruce: But I'll bet it's valuable to be a doctor who has the **whole picture** of how the body works and how to heal it.

Cathy: Yes, in fact, my clinical experience dealing with real patients has been **invaluable** to my research.

Bruce: You must be sick of school though?

30

Cathy: Well, I must admit I've been in school for a long time now. Let's see ... I've been going to school since I was five, and I'm thirty-two now, so I've been in school for twenty-seven years. But, I took this summer off, after I had finished my **dissertation** and completed my oral defense. I had a fabulous time just relaxing at a rented beach house in Cape Cod with some girlfriends.

Bruce: You know, I thought your kidney transplant a few years back would slow you down. But you seem to have an **inexhaustible** supply of energy.

Cathy: Well, my accident forced me to take a **leave of absence** for one **semester**. I was **bored out of my mind** the whole time I was in the hospital. After I had my kidney transplant, I couldn't wait to get back to my research.

Bruce: Are you cured now? I mean, do you have any problems with your kidney?

Cathy: No, in fact, I **feel as good as new**. All I have to show for my accident and operation are a few **scars** on my lower back.

Bruce: I have a lot of admiration for you. I think you were very **gutsy** to bounce right back after your accident. Many people, I think, would have gotten depressed or given up on their goal.

Cathy: Well, I certainly wasn't going to let an accident get in the way of my dream to be a scientist. I've wanted to be one since I was a kid. If anything, I think my accident **heightened** my interest in medicine.

Bruce: What do you mean?

Cathy: Much of my research has been on the cornea and cornea transplants. As an organ **recipient** myself, I have real empathy for those blind people who are in need of transplants.

Bruce: I can believe that . . . So, are you going to take me to your lab?

Cathy: Sure, if you want. I don't think you'll find it all that interesting. It's just a small room with a lot of lab equipment **festooned** around, but I'll take you on a tour of the rest of the research hospital.

Bruce: Now you don't use poor little rabbits or monkeys in your experiments, do you?

Cathy: Don't worry, we only use frogs.

Bruce: Oh, good. I never liked frogs anyway!

DISCUSS

1. Animals are used in medical research to aid in the search for cures to human diseases and **disorders**. Recently there have been protests against what some **perceive** as cruel and inhumane experimenting on these animals. Some argue for limiting animal research, others for **abolishing** it. What do you think?

2. What do you think of organ transplants? The **editorial** at the beginning of this chapter **advocates** an efficient national network for **facilitating** organ transplants. Do you think this is a good idea? If, as the editorial states, the medical and communication technologies necessary for this efficient national network exist today, then why do you think one hasn't been established already?

3. Some of Cathy's research has been on new kinds of **contact lenses** that can be worn for extended periods of time. What are contact lenses? Why do people wear them? Are they popular in your country? What are some of the problems with them? with glasses?

4. As an **undergraduate**, do you think it's better to attend a large research university, like the University of Wisconsin, or a small college? Why?

5. There is no national **health insurance** in the U.S. To be covered under a health insurance plan, you either have to purchase one yourself or receive it as a **benefit** from your employer. Many people are not covered by health insurance at all. How does health insurance work in general? How is health care paid for in your country? Do you think national health insurance is a good idea?

WRITE

In a 125-word essay describe an occasion in which you visited a doctor or went to a hospital. What was wrong with you? What did the doctors do? Were you cured? Were you given treatment or **medication**? Was it a positive or a negative experience?

ACTIVE VOCABULARY REVIEW

The words are in alphabetical order. The definitions are scrambled in each group. AS A GLOSSARY to understand the lesson, find the word alphabetically and select the definition that fits the context. AS AN EXERCISE, write the correct word next to each definition. To save time, you can do the exercise orally in class and then write it as homework.

to abolish:_____ to assign as a share; to distribute

to advocate:_____ insurance, etc. given by an employer

to allocate:_____ to be very bored

benefits:_____ to speak in favor of; to recommend

to be bored out of one's mind:_____ to eliminate; to put an end to

casket:_____ to think about in order to decide

clinician:_____ a box in which a corpse is buried

collective:_____ small, flexible lenses put on the eyes

to consider:_____ taken all together; total

contact lenses:_____ doctor who works in a clinic

cornea:_____ pleasant thought; fancy

cutting-edge:_____ farm where milk, butter, etc. are produced

dairy:_____ transparent outer coat protecting the eyeball

data bank:_____ most advanced

daydream:_____ computer memory with stored information

dental:_____ disease with excessive sugar in the blood

diabetes:_____ research report for the Ph.D. degree

dialysis:_____ abnormal function, infirmity

disorder:_____ a process to purify the blood

dissertation:_____ related to the teeth

to donate:_____ to be completely healed

donor:_____ to make easy; to lessen the work of

editorial:_____ to give voluntarily

to facilitate:_____ person who gives something

to feel as good as new:_____ newspaper statement with the publisher's opinion

to festoon:_____ first-year college student
freshman:_____ of or pertaining to the future
funeral:_____ one who is not a specialist
futuristic:_____ to decorate; to adorn
generalist:_____ ceremonies for the burial of the dead

to greet:_____ to increase; to intensify; to enhance
gutsy [slang]:_____ a plan to cover medical expenses
heartbeat:_____ to address in welcome
health insurance:_____ brave; defiant; courageous
to heighten:_____ pulsation of the heart

inexhaustible:_____ very precious; valuable beyond measure
invaluable:_____ tissue connecting bones and holding organs in place
leave of absence:_____ very abundant; tireless; infinite
ligament:_____ to consider inferior
to look down on:_____ absent from duty with permission

match: _____ substance used to cure or heal; medicine
M.D.: _____ an exact counterpart
medication:_____ the eardrum and cavity with three small bones
middle ear:_____ animal or plant part performing some function
organ: _____ Medical Doctor

to perceive:_____ extremely valuable
Ph.D.: _____ to feel deeply; to apprehend
physician:_____ restored; regenerated
priceless:_____ doctorate degree, doctor of philosophy
recycled:_____ doctor of medicine

rigor: _____ mark left by a healed wound
rolling:_____ to act as a messenger
to run errands: _____ one-half of the school year
scar: _____ severity; strictness; hardship
semester:_____ of land, rising and falling in gentle slopes

to sign up: _____ identification number for retirement
Social Security number: _____ to associate oneself with; to join
specialist: _____ to appear to one
to strike one: _____ cord that connects muscles to the bones
tendon: _____ expert in a particular field of activity

tissue: _____ complete knowledge; total understanding
to transplant: _____ blood vessel carrying blood to the heart
undergraduate: _____ to move an organ from one person to another
vein: _____ student studying for the bachelor's degree
whole picture: _____ substance forming the parts of animals and plants

SPEAK

Cathy: Bruce, you mentioned that you had seen some of our old friends recently. Didn't you say you'd seen Larry in Quebec? How's he doing? Is he married yet? Valerie mentioned in her last letter that she had been to Larry's restaurant while on a visit to Quebec and that Larry had introduced her to his fiancée.

Bruce: He's doing very well. In fact, he's making quite a name for himself as a restauranteur. He isn't married yet, but he told me that he had gotten engaged and was planning to get married soon.

Cathy: I believe his fiancée is French.

Bruce: Yes, she is. Larry told me that they had met some years ago when he was taking a course in France. He said they'd known each other for a long time. By the way, he tried to convince me that I should give up the singles' lifestyle and "settle down."

Cathy: And what did you say to that?

Bruce: I assured him that I had been giving the matter some serious thought. I told him I might even "take the plunge" before he did.

Cathy: Well, Bruce, it's about time! I'm delighted to hear it. By the way, how about Frank and Janet O'Brien? You also saw them recently, didn't you? They seem to be having such a good marriage.

Bruce: Well, they are still happily married, but they told me they had had some very bad luck.

Cathy: Why? What happened?

Bruce: They told me that their dog -- the old German shepherd they'd had for years -- had been killed in an accident, and that they'd been feeling depressed because of that. Then they went on to say that not long after the loss of their dog their house had been broken into and that Janet's jewelry and her family silver had been stolen.

Cathy: Was any of it found?

Bruce: No, none of it was recovered. Janet said that the valuables had been insured and that the insurance company had settled her claim. However, she said that she would never be able to replace the stolen articles because they were antiques.

Cathy: Surely, no more mishaps occurred after that?

Bruce: Actually, there was one more disaster. Janet told me that there had been a terrible storm and that her studio had been flooded. Some of her paintings had been damaged in the flood.

Cathy: The last time I heard from Janet she mentioned that she had been working on paintings for an exhibition. Was she able to restore the damaged paintings?

Bruce: She said she had restored most of them. She told me that she would soon be having an exhibition of her paintings at a well-known New York gallery. In fact, I promised her that I would try to visit her exhibition if I had an opportunity to go to New York.

INDIRECT SPEECH I: STATEMENTS WITH THE VERBS **SAY** AND **TELL**

Larry told me that they had met some years ago in France.

I promised her that I would try to visit her exhibition.

He said that they had known each other for a long time.

Larry suggested to me that I should stay longer.

She told me that she would soon be having an exhibition of her paintings.

She said that she would never be able to replace the stolen articles.

REVIEW

A.   The verbs **SAY** and **TELL** and reported speech.

The verbs **SAY** and **TELL** can both be used to report indirectly what someone has said:

> Cathy said [to Bruce] that she enjoyed her work.
> Cathy told Bruce that she enjoyed her work.

SAY can be immediately followed by a noun clause or by a to + noun or pronoun and then by a noun clause:

> Cathy said that she enjoyed her work.
> Cathy said to Bruce that she enjoyed her work.

SAY is used to quote speech directly:

Cathy said [to Bruce], "I enjoy my work."

TELL is more frequent than **SAY** in reporting speech and is not used for quoting direct speech. **TELL** is followed by an indirect object (noun or pronoun) and then by a noun clause:

Cathy told Bruce that she had become a specialist.

In informal speech **that** is often omitted from noun clauses which follow **say** and **tell**:

Bruce said [that] he wanted to see the research lab.
Cathy told Bruce [that] she would show him the research lab.

Other verbs of indirect speech which follow the pattern of **TELL** (**TELL +** indirect object + **THAT** clause) are: **ASSURE, CONVINCE, INFORM, NOTIFY, PERSUADE, PROMISE, REMIND, TEACH, WARN**:

Cathy told (assured, convinced, informed) Bruce that she had fully recovered from her operation.
She told (warned) him that he might not find the research lab very interesting.

Verbs which follow the pattern of **SAY** (**SAY + TO +** noun or pronoun + **THAT**, clause or which may be immediately followed by a **THAT** clause) are: **ADMIT, ANNOUNCE, BOAST, COMPLAIN, COMMENT, CONFESS, DECLARE, DENY, EXPLAIN, HINT, INDICATE, MENTION, OBSERVE, PROVE, REMARK, REVEAL, REPORT, STATE, SUGGEST, SWEAR**:

You said (indicated, reported, hinted) [to me] that you might be interested in this position.
The lawyer said (proved, announced, declared) [to the jury] that the defendant was innocent.

AGREE / DISAGREE are followed by **WITH +** a noun clause:

Cathy agreed [with Bruce] that her medical training had been very long.

39

I disagree [with you] that doctors should be paid more than other professional people.

B.   Other uses of **TELL**.

TELL is used in expressions such as: **TELL THE TRUTH / A LIE, TELL A STORY / A JOKE / THE FACTS / THE NEWS, TELL THE TIME, TELL THE DIFFERENCE.**   An indirect object usually follows an expression of this kind:

My friend was always telling us jokes.
Did May tell you the good news?

TELL (= give information orally) + indirect object + **ABOUT** (experiences / ideas / plans / objects):

John told us about his trip to Africa.
Please tell me about your plans.

TALK and **SPEAK** are used to refer to oral communication but they are not used to report speech.

SPEAK / TALK + (to someone) + (about something / someone):

Cathy and Bruce talked for hours.
John spoke at length about his plans for the future.
I talked to a lot of people at the cocktail party.
Bruce and Cathy talked about their old friends.

SPEAK may be used to mean "give a speech" or to refer to the manner of language in which a person speaks:

The President will speak on T.V. tonight.
A politician must speak well in order to convince his listeners.
Few Americans speak Japanese.

VOCABULARY VARIATIONS

He's doing very well.
He's making a very good living.
He's been quite successful.

He's making quite a name for himself.
He's becoming well-known / famous.
He is building up a considerable reputation for himself.

I had been giving the matter [some serious thought.
                                              [my earnest consideration.
I had been thinking seriously about that subject.
I had been considering the matter.

I told him [I might "take the plunge" before he did.
                 [I might "tie the knot" before her did.
                 [I might get married before he did.

They went on to say that . . .
They added that . . .
They continued to tell me that . . .

It's about time!
It's high time!
It's none too soon!

PRACTICE

A.   Change the direct speech in the following sentences to reported speech:

Example: "I am thinking about getting engaged," Bruce said.
                      Bruce said that he was thinking about getting engaged.

1.   "I don't want to leave now but I must.
                Dan said that he

2. "I am going to tell you the truth about the incident."
    Barbara promised her lawyer

3. "I may not be able to come here this afternoon, but I'll try to come tomorrow."
    Bruce said to his friends that

4. "I saw our old friends Frank and Janet last week."
    Bruce told Cathy that

5. "I can't cope with these problems any more; I need help."
    Valerie admitted to her psychiatrist that she

6. "You have an appointment at 9:00 A.M. tomorrow."
    The doctor reminded Larry that he

7. "You can depend on my support, Mr. President."
    The National Security Advisor assured the President that he

8. "If you don't make your mortgage payments on time we will have to charge you a late payment fee."
    The loan officer warned us that if we

9. "I have made many serious mistakes, and I don't want to repeat them."
    Bruce confessed to his old friend that

10. "I have put on a lot of weight; I must go on a diet."
    Larry declared that

B.   Change from reported speech to direct speech:

Example: The teacher said he was too tired to go on the trip with us.
          The teacher said, "I'm too tired to go on the trip with you."

1.   The police officer asked the young man where he lived.

2.   The elderly lady asked what time it was.

3.   The instructor told his students to put down their pens.

4.   My host asked me whether I liked living in Washington, D.C.?

5.   Ann said we couldn't get on the bus because it was too crowded.

6.   The tourist asked us whether we could tell him where the metro station was.

7.   She said she had flown from Paris to New York many times.

8.   He told the children to turn off the lights before they went to bed.

9.   Ann said that she would meet him later.

10.   Peter said that he had visited all the museums.

C. Choose the correct words in the following sentences.
Cross out the incorrect words:

1. He **said / told** me that I should return the next day.

2. George Washington **said / told** "I cannot tell a lie."

3. I hope that you will **say / tell** the truth.

4. My investment consultant **said / told** me some interesting facts about that company.

5. Can you **say / tell** me the time, please?

6. Bruce **told / said** to Janet that he might go to the art exhibition.

7. I can't **say / tell** the difference between Coke and Pepsi.

8. I am not good at **telling / saying** jokes.

9. Toshi **talks / speaks** English without accent.

10. The Republican candidate will **speak / talk** at the political rally.

Justice, the law, and a lawyer

Unit   4

MINNEAPOLIS

What to Do in a Traffic Accident

Most traffic accidents can be prevented by following good driving habits, **obeying** all traffic laws and customs, and keeping alert for any changes in traffic or road conditions. However, there are some situations where a **crash** is unavoidable.

When Involved in a Crash

When you are personally involved in a traffic accident, you should take care to follow these **guidelines** at the scene of the accident:

-- Stop at once and give aid to anyone injured in the crash.

-- Call the proper law enforcement agency (as listed below), and an **ambulance** if necessary.

-- Get the names and addresses of all persons involved in the crash and any **witnesses** who come forward.

-- Furnish the name and address of the insurance company which provides your car's **liability** insurance coverage to anyone involved in the accident who requests the information. You must also give the name of your local insurance agent. If you don't have this information with you, you must provide it within 72 hours. State law requires that every driver must carry **proof** that the vehicle the person is driving is currently covered by insurance. The Commissioner of Public Safety may **suspend** the driver's license of anyone who does not provide this proof.

-- If you are involved in a traffic accident which results in injuries or death, you are required by law to report the accident promptly to local authorities.

-- In cases of injury or death, to total property damage amounting to $500 or more, a written report must be sent to the Commissioner of Public Safety, St. Paul, MN 55155, by all drivers involved. This report must be filed within 10 days after the accident has occurred.

-- If your vehicle hits a vehicle which is **unoccupied**, you must either report it to the police, make an attempt to locate the vehicle's owner, or leave a written note in an obvious place. Make sure the note includes your name and address.

-- If your vehicle damages any other kind of property, make sure you inform the property owner what happened.

Remember, you must stop whenever you are involved in a crash. You must also show your driver's license and give your name, address, and vehicle registration number to other people involved. This rule applies to any type of accident.

Your driver's license may be SUSPENDED for not reporting an accident as required by Minnesota law. Accident reports help the Minnesota Department of Public Safety evaluate traffic accidents which occur on Minnesota roadways. This allows them to make changes which will improve road and traffic conditions within this state. Your report is CONFIDENTIAL and cannot be used against you in any court of law.

Witnessing and Reporting an Accident

You should report any traffic accidents which you witness. Any injuries or deaths which result from a traffic accident must be reported by the quickest **means** available -- usually a telephone. The best means of getting the information to the proper agency is to dial 911 on the telephone. In areas that aren't served by 911, dial the operator and ask for ZENITH 7000. This will put you in touch with the closest State Patrol office. They will then contact the proper enforcement agency to handle the accident.

When reporting a crash, and asking for aid, be sure to give the exact location, how much damage was involved and any injuries or deaths which resulted from the accident.

Accuracy is very important. It helps police respond more quickly and efficiently. To insure the best possible handling of the situation, all crashes should be reported to the law enforcement agency which has **jurisdiction** (legal authority) over the area where the accident happened.

NARRATIVE

Bruce had thought of the Midwest as flat, grey and boring. So he is once again surprised by another **delightful** Midwestern city: Minneapolis. With friend Vincent Belanger as tour guide, Bruce tours the length and **breadth** of town. He takes in the beautiful lakes and parks, the **bustling** commercial district, the diverse ethnic neighborhoods, the university and library, and the **dazzling** nightlife. The city seems to be a model city -- **charming,** safe, clean, with good public services and a rich cultural life. Bruce is most impressed, however, by the friendliness of the people. He's never been in a more **amicable** city. Wondering whether or not he's in **Utopia**, Bruce queries Vinnie, a lawyer, as they bicycle around one of the city's lakes.

DIALOGUE

Bruce: From all I've seen here, I'm almost convinced to drop everything and move to Minneapolis.

Vinnie: Many people say it has one of the highest qualities of life of any city in the country.

Bruce: But there must be an **Achilles' heel**, a dark side to the city which I'm not seeing.

Vinnie: Certainly, like any major modern city, we have our share of problems.

Bruce: Such as . . . ?

Vinnie: Crime, drugs, unemployment, homelessness, et cetera. We just seem to have a little less of them than other cities.

Bruce: I guess you get to see your share of the problems when you're in court?

Vinnie: It's true. All life's big problems seem to end up in court sooner of later.

Bruce: What kind of work are you doing now?

Vinnie: I'm a defense lawyer. Right now, I'm working on a big case which is getting a lot of **media publicity**.

Bruce: Who are you defending?

Vinnie: A guy who's being prosecuted on drunk driving charges. He hit a pedestrian who is now **paralyzed** for life.

Bruce: Oh! That's terrible. So if the guy did it, why are you defending him? Shouldn't the bad guys always go to jail?

Vinnie: Well, an important part of our judicial system is the right to **due process** and a fair **trial**.

Bruce: But how can you defend this guy?

Vinnie: Our legal system is **emulated** the world over precisely because it is extremely fair and allows everyone the right to counsel.

Bruce: I guess you're right. Too many countries have **kangaroo courts**. I just think that drunk drivers -- if they truly are guilty -- should go to jail.

50

Vinnie: You'd make a good **prosecutor**!
            (They both laugh)

Vinnie: But seriously, you will be happy to know that most states have recently
            enacted tougher laws against drunk drivers.

Bruce: Good . . . Say, let's **take a break** from this bicycling. I'm **not in
            shape**.

DISCUSS

1. How does one get permission to drive in your country? What sort of training is
    required? Can you drive? If so, offer some safety tips -- which you may have
    learned from experience -- to a novice driver.

2. U.S. jurisprudence has indeed been emulated around the world. There is a **motto**
    which summarizes one of the founding principles of this system: Better to allow a
    thousand guilty men to go free than to let one innocent one **rot** in jail. Do you
    agree? Should the accused have rights?

3. What are the attitudes in your country toward drunk driving? What happens to
    drunk drivers if they are caught?

4. Automobiles are an American passion. It is every American kid's dream to own a
    sleek sports car. In today's increasingly congested and polluted cities, however,
    public transportation is a crying need. Do you drive or take public transit? Which
    is better? How would the two be balanced against each other in an ideal society?

5. Drugs are a problem in the world's major cities. What's the solution?

WRITE

Here's a description of a crime: A nineteen-year-old man has **shoplifted** a gold
bracelet from a jewelry store. He is apprehended a block away from the store by the police
and caught with the stolen object in his pocket. He is arrested and charged with **larceny**,
a **felony**. This is the young man's first arrest. Choose to be either the prosecuting
attorney or the defense attorney. In a 125-word essay, present your case to the judge.
Recommend a **sentence**.

ACTIVE VOCABULARY REVIEW

The words are in alphabetical order. The definitions are scrambled in each group. AS A GLOSSARY to understand the lesson, find the word alphabetically and select the definition that fits the context. AS AN EXERCISE, write the correct word next to each definition. To save time, you can do the exercise orally in class and then write it as homework.

accuracy:_____ a weak, vulnerable point

Achilles' heel:_____ friendly; peaceable

ambulance:_____ distance across; width

amicable:_____ a vehicle equipped to transport the sick or wounded

breadth: _____ condition of being without mistakes; exactness

bustling:_____ having an attractive, friendly personality

charming:_____ collision; accident

crash: _____ amazing, bright, and active

dazzling:_____ giving pleasure; enjoyable

delightful:_____ noisily busy; very active

due: _____ a suggestion for a future course of action

to emulate:_____ proper; rightful; suitable

to enact:_____ a very serious crime

felony:_____ to carry out in action

guideline:_____ to try to equal or surpass

in shape [informal]:_____ illegal, unfair court

jurisdiction:_____ unlawful taking of someone's property; theft

kangaroo court:_____ state of being under obligation; responsibility

larceny:_____ power of administering justice

liability:_____ in good physical condition

manual: _____ newspapers, magazines, radio, T.V., etc.

means: _____ to follow a law or a rule

media [plural]:_____ expression telling a guiding principle

motto: _____ the agency, method of doing something

to obey: _____ a booklet explaining how something works

52

paralyzed:_____ whatever clarifies the truth or falsehood of...

process:_____ unable to move

proof: _____ action at law

prosecutor:_____ process of getting public attention

publicity:_____ one who accuses a person for criminal offenses

to rot: _____ to steal from a store

sentence:_____ to become spoiled, bad

to shoplift:_____ to hold back temporarily

sleek: _____ decision on a punishment given by a judge

to suspend: _____ neat; elegant; chic

to take a break:_____ a perfect society without problems

trial: _____ vacant; idle

unoccupied:_____ person who gives testimony in court

Utopia: _____ the process to determine guilt or innocence

witness:_____ to rest for a short time

SPEAK

Brian has just returned home from a day at the beach. He is visibly upset.

Brian: Boy, I could really do with a drink. Today has been a rough one.

Wendy: You've had a change of mood since you left this morning. What brought that about?

Brian: I had an accident on the way back from the beach.

Wendy: Oh, no! What happened? Are you all right?

Brian: Yes, I'm fine, but I'm so mad. It hasn't even sunk in yet.

Wendy: What happened? Tell me from the beginning. Were you in the right or the wrong? Is the car badly damaged?

Brian: Yes. And no, I wasn't in the wrong at all. I was heading for home after a good day at the beach. I was on the highway going below the speed limit when all of a sudden the driver of the car on my left decided that he wanted to take the exit that we were just about to pass. So he tried to pass in front of me! I slammed on my brakes, but it was too late and I ran into him. Clearly it was his fault.

Wendy: What happened then?

Brian: Well, I immediately started to pull over. Fortunately, there was no one behind me.

Wendy: Was the other guy okay?

Brian: Okay? Okay? He didn't even stop!

Wendy: No!

Brian: Yes! I'm not making this up. Luckily, I was able to make out his license number, and I wrote it down on a piece of paper, so now I can follow it up.

Wendy: How awful! Who'll pay for the damages? You can't let him get off scot-free.

Brian: I know. I actually went after him to pay him back; I was so furious.

Wendy: I can't believe it! You didn't!

Brian: But he was in a much faster car, so I had to give up.

Wendy: Brian, you're crazy! They could put you away for that kind of crazy behavior.

Brian: I know. I was in a rage -- I guess it's wearing off now. I'm going to call up the police.

Wendy: Yes, that's the thing to do. Call them up right now. They'll probably ask you to go down to the station to fill out a few forms. Can I get you a drink while you calm down?

Brian: Yes, please. I'd love a rum and coke.

Wendy: Maybe you should have just the coke. I'm sure the police will pick up the fact that you smell of alcohol.

PHRASAL VERBS

Boy, I could really <u>do with</u> a drink.

What <u>brought</u> that <u>about</u>?

Well, I immediately started to <u>pull over</u>.

REVIEW

Phrasal verbs are made up of a simple verb plus a preposition or a particle.

e.g.   Do + with   I <u>could do with</u> a drink.
       Sink + in   It <u>hasn't sunk in</u> yet.

55

They are also called two-word verbs or three-word verbs. These verbs function just like any other verbs, in all tenses, in the active and passive voices and as transitive or intransitive (or both) verbs.

Some phrasal verbs have their own idiomatic meaning.

e.g.   You can't let him <u>get off</u> scott-free.
        You can't let him <u>escape without any punishment</u>.

Some are less formal equivalents of already existing verbs.

e.g.   I <u>ran into</u> your sister on the street yesterday.
        I <u>met</u> your sister on the street yesterday.

And some merely serve to extend the meaning of the verb.

e.g.   I was able to make out his license number, and I <u>wrote</u> it <u>down</u> on a piece of paper.
        I was able to make out his license number, and I <u>wrote</u> it on a piece of paper.

Correct usage involves knowing which phrasal verbs take which prepositions/particles, which phrasal verbs can be separated, and when, for the purposes of style, they should not be separated.

Phrasal verbs can be divided into two categories: separable and non-separable.

<u>Separable phrasal verbs</u> may take the direct object before or after the preposition/particle. However, the direct object pronoun <u>must</u> come <u>before</u> the preposition/particle.

e.g.   The police <u>followed</u> the case <u>up</u>.
or   The police <u>followed up</u> the case.
        The police <u>followed</u> it <u>up</u>.

"The police <u>followed up</u> it." is not correct because <u>follow up</u> is a separable phrasal verb and so must be separated if the direct object is a pronoun.

<u>Non-separable phrasal verbs</u> on the other hand cannot be separated at any time. Both direct objects and direct object pronouns must follow the preposition/particle.

e.g.   They couldn't <u>get around</u> the problem.
or   They couldn't <u>get around</u> it.

"They couldn't <u>get</u> it <u>around</u>." is incorrect because <u>get around</u> is a non-separable phrasal verb.

In order to use phrasal verbs correctly, it is helpful to think of the idiomatic verbs as less formal than their one-word counterparts and use them according to the context. For example, "I actually <u>went after</u> him to <u>pay</u> him <u>back</u>." is more natural than "I actually chased him to get my revenge." because the context is informal.

In addition, separable phrasal verbs tend not to be separated by long direct objects even though it is grammatically correct.

e.g.   I'll <u>pay back</u> the man who ran into me and didn't stop.
       I'll <u>pay</u> him <u>back</u>

Both examples above are acceptable, but "I'll <u>pay</u> the man who ran into me and didn't stop <u>back</u>." is not."

VOCABULARY VARIATIONS

Today has been a tough one.
Today has been a disaster / a fiasco / hell.

You've had a change of mood.
You're in a different mood.
You've had quite a mood swing.

Brian, you're crazy! [insane! / mad!
                     [a lunatic!
                     [out of your mind!

PRACTICE

A.   Change the direct objects to direct object pronouns. Remember to separate the verb if it is separable.

  1.   I was heading for the football field when I heard the news.

  2.   Have you noticed that Bruce always smells of cologne?

  3.   Lawyers often have to follow up boring cases.

  4.   You have the right to call up a lawyer if you're arrested.

57

5. Legal proceedings often involve filling out many forms.

6. The child always forgot to put away his toys.

7. The mother picks up her children on her way back home.

8. We ran into our class-mates at the swimming pool.

9. The police officer blew his whistle for us to get off the grass.

10. I could do with a slice of that cake.

B. Correct the following sentences.

1. We ran John into this morning on the way to work.

2. Brian actually made the story about being in a hit-and-run accident up.

3. I know that revenge is immature, but I really wanted to pay her for what she had done to me.

4. Linda needs a relaxing weekend badly. She could really do one with.

5. I have news that will affect the prosecutor's case. I'll call up her.

6. The interviewer told the applicants to fill the application forms.

7. It was so dark that she couldn't see the number of the house. She couldn't make out it.

8. They have a part-time job available at Hardee's. I'm going it after.

9. He was exhausted, but he didn't want to give up it.

10. Here are my telephone number and address. Write down them, please.

C. Match the idiomatic phrasal verbs in column A with their equivalents in column B. Then use five of them in original sentences of your own.

	A			**B**
make up	_____	1	get revenge
bring about	_____	2	put in prison
go after	_____	3	cause to happen
fill out	_____	4	see
call up	_____	5	investigate
pay back	_____	6	telephone
follow up	_____	7	complete
make out	_____	8	invent
put away	_____	9	collide with
run into	_____	10	chase

Sentences:

1. _____
    _____ .

2. _____
    _____ .

3. _____
    _____ .

4. _____
    _____ .

5. _____
    _____ .

Cape Kennedy: The Space Shuttle

R.L.

Unit 5

CAPE KENNEDY, FLORIDA

U.S. NEWS & WORLD REPORT, Sept. 26, 1988

A LUNAR OBSERVATORY

On the far side of the moon, free of the electronic **clamor** from Earth, **astronauts** could **deploy** telescopes **to relay spectacular** views of the universe to **terrestrial** scientists.

The far side of Earth's moon is extraordinarily clear and quiet. There is no **atmosphere**, and the land doesn't shake. The moon itself is a massive **shield** against the growing electronic clamor **emanating** from Earth. It is quite possibly the best location in the entire **solar system** for **optical** and **radio telescopes**, and **NASA** is exploring how to take advantage of it.

Building and operating an observatory on the side of the moon facing away from Earth could combine the **drama** of human space flight with the promise of high scientific **yield**. Like early **Antarctic** scientific outposts, the station would not be permanently inhabited, though astronauts would visit it two weeks a year to perform experiments, study the lunar **geology** and make repairs on the observatory's automatic systems.

The lunar observatory's job would be to gather incredibly **high-resolution** views of the universe across the radio and optical spectrums. To accomplish this, astronauts would erect dozens of small radio-receiving **antennas** and mirrors across 10 to 15 miles of the **bleak** lunar landscape. Signals picked up by each antenna would be sent to a moon-based computer, which would **integrate** them into one image. The effect would be the same as if one gigantic single mirror or antenna had been deployed, instead of many.

NARRATIVE

Bruce hurries from Minneapolis to Orlando, Florida by plane to **catch** the launching of the **space shuttle**. His friend Ralph Mendez, who works for NASA, has invited him down to **Cape Kennedy** to watch the **launch**. Ralph is a **technician** who works on the shuttle's **booster rockets** and, thus, has **ringside seats** for the events. He gets a visitor's **pass** for Bruce to come into the command and control center.

There are still three hours left in the **countdown**, so Ralph takes a break from his work and joins Bruce for a cup of coffee in the observation room. Far across the **tarmac** they can see the majestic space shuttle **Discovery**. It sits **poised**, strapped vertically to the back of a powerful red booster rocket. By now the astronauts have entered the shuttle's **cockpit**, and there is a **tingling** feeling of **anticipation** in the air.

DIALOGUE

Bruce: I'm surprised you are able to take a break this close to **lift off**, Ralph.

Ralph: Well, most of our work is done at this point. The only thing we have to do now is **monitor** the computers in case of a **malfunction**. If there is a problem, I'll be **paged** over the **P.A.** system.

Bruce: Everyone seems so calm. I thought it would be **frantic** in here during countdown.

Ralph: No, at this point the computers have taken over. The only thing humans do is to decide, if and when a problem occurs, whether or not to **scrap** the countdown.

Bruce: What happens if the countdown is scrapped?

Ralph: Well, then we have to find the problem, fix it and reschedule the launch. Often the window of time in which we can launch is very small.

Bruce: Why is that?

Ralph: Well, for example, this space shuttle is carrying a multi-million dollar space **probe** which will travel billions of miles into the solar system. In order to travel that distance, the probe uses what is called "the **slingshot** effect." This means that it will use the gravitational fields of the big planets to "throw" it further into space; the same way a stone is **slung** out of a slingshot.

Bruce: So, what does that have to do with the fact that the shuttle can only be launched within a short period of time?

Ralph: Right. Well, the planets have to be in the right position in order for the probe to utilize them. So, **concretely**, if we don't get the Discovery launched by next Tuesday, then we'll have to wait 18 months, until the planets are in the correct position again.

Bruce: I see. I hadn't realized how complicated this whole procedure was. And what is this space probe on the Discovery going to do?

Ralph: Once the Discovery is in **orbit** around the earth, it will release the probe at a specified point. The probe will take several years traveling at high speeds to reach the **asteroid** belt. Once there, it will take both optical and **infrared** pictures and collect other data. It will also orbit around **Neptune** and collect data about that planet.

Bruce: So the release of this space probe is a key element of the space shuttle's mission, but I was under the impression that the astronauts in the shuttle would be performing some experiments themselves.

Ralph: You're absolutely correct. The release of the probe is only one of many tasks. In addition, the astronauts will be conducting a number of scientific experiments that require a weightless environment, including some in which they themselves act as **guinea pigs** .

Bruce: What do you mean?

Ralph: There are medical experiments in which the astronauts take part. Their **vital signs** are monitored by doctors and medical teams back on earth. One that I know about involves seeing how blood will **clot** in space.

Bruce: Wow, I've really learned a lot. For some reason I thought all the shuttle's missions were **top secret**. I never really knew what the space shuttles actually did.

Ralph: Well, some of the launches are top secret. They involve sensitive military testing. Even technicians like myself have no idea what the mission is about. This particular mission, however, is not **classified** .

Bruce: Yes, I guess they wouldn't allow a soap opera actor like myself to observe a secret operation. Who knows, I could be a Russian **spy** !

DISCUSS

1. Bruce jokes about being a Russian spy. What do you thing about spies? Are they necessary? Why or why not? How did Gorbachev's policy of **glasnost** and the downfall of Communism in the former Soviet Union affect **espionage** and the **Cold War** in general?

2. There is a fierce debate amongst those interested in space exploration over whether resources should be concentrated on **manned** or unmanned space flights.

3. Since the beginning of human history there has been speculation about **extraterrestrial** life. Many legends, books and movies tell of **Martians, UFOs, aliens** and **flying saucers**. One of the most popular American T.V. shows of all time, "Star Trek," is about humans who, while exploring and patrolling space, meet up with an assortment of creatures from other planets. Recently, some scientists, including Dr. Carl Sagan of Cornell University, have asserted there is a very good chance that life exists in other parts of the universe. What do you think? Is there extraterrestrial life? Are we ever likely to meet it? What would it be like?

4. Not far from the Kennedy Space Center is **Disney World**. There are now Disney Worlds in Europe, Japan and Kuwait. Describe what Disney World is like, from what you know. Describe other **amusement parks** and their **rides** and attractions.

5. From what your know and have learned, how did the universe begin? When?

WRITE

You are the director of NASA. In a 125-word essay describe a space project (the reading at the beginning of this chapter is one example) you would like to **undertake**. What are your goals? How would you do it?

ACTIVE VOCABULARY REVIEW

The words are in alphabetical order. The definitions are scrambled in each group. AS A GLOSSARY to understand the lesson, find the word alphabetically and select the definition that fits the context. AS AN EXERCISE, write the correct word next to each definition. To save time, you can do the exercise orally in class and then write it as homework.

alien:_____ park with recreational rides: roller coaster, Ferris Wheel, etc.

amusement park:_____ aerial for transmitting or receiving radio waves

Antarctica:_____ creature from outer space

antenna: _____ act of realizing in advance; expectation

anticipation:_____ continent around the South Pole

asteroid belt:_____ rocket that sends a spacecraft up into space

astronauts: _____ group of small planets between Mars and Jupiter

atmosphere:_____ cold, harsh and gloomy

bleak: _____ people who explore space

booster rocket:_____ the layer of gases around a planet

Cape Kennedy:_____ a loud noise

to catch [slang]:_____ when blood forms into lumps

clamor:_____place in Florida where rockets are launched into space

classified:_____ to watch; to see

to clot:_____ secret, for the military

cockpit:_____ to put in place; to install

Cold War: _____ in reality; actually

concretely:__ checking the rocket before launch to the final seconds, 10,9,8,7...

countdown:_____ hostile relations between the U.S. and the U.S.S.R.

to deploy:_____ where the pilots sit and fly the plane

Disney World:_____ to come forth; to arise; to emerge

drama: _____ not from the planet Earth

to emanate:_____ large amusement park in Florida

espionage:_____ excitement; emotion; tension

extraterrestrial:_____ spying

flying saucer:_____ agitated; frenetic; overexcited

frantic:_____ small animals used in scientific experiments

geology:_____ Gorbachev's policy of openness in the Soviet Union

glascost:_____ a spaceship not from Earth

guinea pigs:_____ science of the Earth's history and composition

high-resolution:_____ invisible rays beyond the red of the spectrum

human race:_____ to bring together; to make into a whole

infrared:_____ human beings; people; mankind

to integrate:_____ to send forth with some force

to launch:_____ very clear; accurate; precise

lift-off:_____ having to do with the moon

lunar:_____ when a rocket goes up; "blast off"

malfunction:_____ imaginary creature from Mars

manned:_____ something which has broken or gone wrong

Martian:_____ furnished with men

to monitor:_____ place with a telescope for observing heavenly bodies

NASA:_____ a planet

Nepture:_____ instrument used to make distant objects appear larger

observatory:_____ National Aeronautics and Space Administration

optical telescope:_____ to watch, observe closely

orbit:_____ to call someone's name over loudspeakers

P.A. system:_____ path of one heavenly body around another

to page:_____ balanced

pass:_____ public address system

poised:_____ permit to pass; a free ticket

probe:_____ rides on roller coasters, bumper cars, etc.

proponent:_____ to pass on a message

radio telescope:_____ device to get information about something

to relay:_____ a device using radio waves to observe space

rides:_____ advocate, a person in favor of a thing

ringside seat:_____ protective device, barrier
robot: _____ to discard or terminate
to scrap: _____ to throw; hurl; fling
shield:_____ mechanical device which performs human functions
to sling:_____ seat with a good view

slingshot:_____ the sun and the planets
solar system:_____ unusual to a striking degree
space shuttle:_____ person who gets secret information for a hostile party
spectacular:_____ device used for shooting stones
spy: _____ a space ship with wings that flies back to Earth

tarmac: _____ exciting; thrilling
technician:_____ having to do with the Earth
terrestrial:_____ runway
tingling:_____ maximum secrecy
top secret:_____ person who works with technical material

UFO: _____ quantity of things produced
to undertake:_____ to raise to a higher level
to uplift:_____ to take a task upon oneself
vital signs:_____ unidentified flying object
yield:_____ pulse, respiration, and temperature

SPEAK

It is Career Orientation Week at Woodbrook High School. Two seniors, Elizabeth and Bill, are talking after a presentation on aerospace studies given by a NASA recruiter.

Elizabeth: So what did you think of that stimulating presentation, Bill? Would you consider becoming an astronaut now that you have an idea of how rewarding and challenging it can be?

Bill: I've always been fascinated by space, Elizabeth, but there's so much that we don't know. I'm not very attracted by the idea because the thought of being in danger, or lost in space, is frightening to me.

Elizabeth: Oh Bill, being an astronaut could be no more dangerous than certain other professions. For example, being a stunt-man could be just as dangerous as being an astronaut, and as exciting. In both cases you simply have to be highly trained to avoid danger.

Bill: Yes, I suppose you're right. In any case, the stringent physical requirements exclude me. I would be limited by my poor eyesight. I don't think I could even fly a plane -- my eyesight is so bad. What about you? Are you interested?

Elizabeth: Yes, I am. I'm even more interested now after listening to the female astronaut talk about her career. Her experiences as a jet-pilot, then as an astronaut, were really impressive.

Bill: Yes, I agree, but even though women aren't as oppressed as they used to be, they still have a difficult time entering male-dominated fields like aerospace studies.

Elizabeth: I know. When I was young, I used to be mesmerized by stars magnified through a telescope. I thought of becoming an astronaut, and one day I told my mother so. Since she was a very conservative woman, she suggested that I become a flight attendant instead, because astronauts were men. As a child I believed her, so I was only discouraged by her advice. Now, I think I would be offended if someone said that to me.

Bill:	True, but you must admit that some of the tasks performed by the astronauts are physically exhausting.
Elizabeth:	Yes, and I'm exhausted only after running a mile! I guess if I want to be an astronaut, I would have to get in shape.
Bill:	You're really inspired, aren't you?
Elizabeth:	Yes ... or confused.
Bill:	Really. Deciding on a career is confusing.

DISTINCTION BETWEEN STATIVE AND DYNAMIC ADJECTIVES

So what did you think of that <u>stimulating</u> presentation, Bill?

I've always been <u>fascinated</u> by space.

Her experiences as a jet-pilot, then as an astronaut, were really <u>impressive</u>.

I used to be <u>mesmerized</u> by stars magnified through a telescope.

REVIEW

Certain verbs can become adjectives with two different forms and two different meanings. They are called <u>stative</u> and <u>dynamic</u> adjectives.

Most dynamic adjectives are formed by adding "-ing" to the verb.
e.g. *Stimulating*. So what did you think of that *stimulating* presentation, Bill?
The dynamic adjective had the meaning of "the feeling or reaction caused."
e.g. The film was *frightening*.

Most stative adjectives are formed by adding "-ed" to the verb.
e.g. *Stimulated.* I was *stimulated* by the presentation.

The stative adjective often has the meaning of "the emotional state of the person(s) experiencing the feeling."
e.g. I was *frightened* by the film.

70

The dynamic adjective is often used with impersonal subjects, whereas the stative adjective is used with personal subjects.

e.g. Elizabeth's mother's advice was *discouraging*.

Elizabeth was *discouraged* by her mother's advice.

There is a small group of verbs which can become stative and dynamic adjectives. In this case, however, the dynamic adjectives use "-ive" instead of "-ing" as the ending.

e.g. Offensive / offended, oppressive / oppressed, attractive / attracted, impressive / impressed, repressive / repressed.

e.g. Her experiences as a jet-pilot, then as an astronaut, were really *impressive*.

I was *impressed* by her experiences.

Usually when the stative adjective is used, a preposition and the agent causing the reaction follow.

e.g. I've always been *fascinated* by space.

She was *bored* with grammar.

When the dynamic adjective is used, either the preposition "to" or "for" and the indirect object follow.

e.g. Space is *fascinating to* me.

Grammar was *boring for* her.

VOCABULARY VARIATIONS

Would you consider] becoming an astronaut?
Would you think of]

I'm not very attracted by] the idea.
I don't particularly like]

The stringent physical requirements] exclude me.
The high physical standards   ]

Here are some of the words from the dialogue defined for you:

recruiter -- someone who enlists the services of others

aerospace -- having to do with the earth's atmosphere and outer space

stringent -- strict and demanding

71

PRACTICE

A.   Choose the appropriate word.

e.g. The puppy's clumsy little movements were <u>amusing</u>/amused.

1.   That documentary on mental illness was <u>depressing</u>/depressed.
2.   I was <u>touched</u>/touching by a letter from my five-year-old.
3.   I find those ethnic jokes offended/<u>offensive</u>.
4.   Her history of lying is <u>shocking</u>/shocked.
5.   I was amazing/<u>amazed</u> by the size of the microchip.
6.   The <u>burning</u>/burned issue of the day is preserving the environment.
7.   The <u>fired</u>/firing worker had to move to another city.
8.   The <u>exhausting</u>/exhausted climb to the mountain peak finally came to an end.
9.   The <u>unsuspecting</u>/unsuspected monkeys were caught in the net.
10.   The damaging/<u>damaged</u> car could not be repaired.

B.   Rewrite the following sentences by changing the stative adjective to the dynamic and the dynamic to the stative.

e.g.   The aerospace studies presentation was stimulating to Elizabeth.
       Elizabeth was stimulated by the aerospace studies presentation.

1.   The tasks performed by the astronauts are physically exhausting.

2.   Bill was not attracted by the idea of being an astronaut.

3.   Bill's poor eyesight is limiting to him.

4.   The female astronaut was inspiring for Elizabeth.

5.   I was mystified by his peculiar behavior.

6.   The grades received by the students were annoying.

7.   The image the dog saw of himself in the water was puzzling.

8.   The news heard on T.V. by the athletes was exciting.

9.   The service the passengers were rendered in the hotel **was satisfying.**

10.   To see so much beauty was surprising to him.

C.   Answer the following questions.   Try to use both forms of the adjective.
e.g.   What do you find offensive?
        I am offended by people smoking cigarettes near me.
        I find people smoking cigarettes near me offensive.

1.   What is frightening to you?

2.   What do you find impressive about space travel?

3.   What do you find annoying about children?

4.   What were you fascinated by as a child?

5.   What is confusing to you in English?

6.   What is insulting to you?

7.   What do you think is surprising about his victory?

8.   What do you find attractive about jogging?

9.   Why do you believe baseball is exciting?

10.   Why do you consider the result disappointing?

Unemployed

Unit 6

NEW ORLEANS
Unemployed

Résumé

JOHN ANDREW HUBBARD
1092 39th **St., Apt. #7**
New Orleans, LA 82109
(504) 346-9216

EDUCATION: Georgetown University
Washington, D.C.
Bachelor of Arts, June 1979
Major: English with a **concentration** in journalism

Honors: Dean's List
Graduated with honors **cum laude**
Butler Essay Prize **recipient**

WORK
EXPERIENCE: SENIOR **COPY EDITOR** 1988 - Present
New Orleans Times Picayune, New Orleans, Louisiana
Supervised staff of copy editors. Wrote **headlines** and
photo captions, worked on **page layout, edited copy.**

COPY EDITOR 1985 - 1988
Atlanta Constitution Atlanta, Georgia
Proofread and **edited** copy **submitted** by journalists. Worked
using personal computers. Worked in **high-pressure** environment
with many **deadlines.**

LANGUAGE TEACHER 1983 - 1985
Instituto de ingles, Montrevideo, Uruguay
Taught English to speaers of Spanish. Developed lesson plans and
teaching tools.

MERCHANT SEAMAN 1980 - 1983
Pan-American Shipping Lines, New York, N.Y.
Worked in the **deck department** as Ordinary **Seaman**
and **Boatswain**. Worked on **tankers** and **freighters** sailing to
ports in North and South America.

RESEARCH ASSISTANT 1979 - 1980
Lado International College, Washington, D.C. Assisted in the writing
of textbooks for English as a second language. Wrote, edited and
proofread **manuscripts**. Developed student exercises.

ACTIVITIES AND
INTERESTS: New Orleans **Amateur** Soccer League player. **Volunteer** English
tutor for refugees

REFERENCES
Available upon request.

NARRATIVE

After the shuttle launch, Bruce spends time with Ralph and his family. They visit
Disney World, Epcot Center, and Sea World. Although he enjoys these renowned tourist
attractions, three days of waiting in lines, listening to screaming children and looking at
displays is enough for Bruce; he is ready to move on.

Bruce flies to New Orleans and is met at the airport by his college classmate, Andy
Hubbard. Andy does not look well. He has bags under his eyes, his hair is rumpled and
he is unshaven. Bruce, looking tanned and relaxed, greets his frazzled friend with a big
hug. Bruce has already dined on the plane so they decide to throw Bruce's bag in the back
of the car and to drive straight to a blues club to have a drink, hear some music and talk.

DIALOGUE

Bruce: Let's sit over here, away from the stage so the music won't be so loud and we
           can talk.

Andy: Sounds good to me.

Waiter: Can I get you something to drink?

Andy: Get me a **double Scotch.**

Bruce: I'll have a **draft beer.**

Andy: You know, it's really good to see you, Bruce.

Bruce: It's good to see you, too, Andy. You look like you've been going through a **rough time.** Tell me about it.

Andy: Well, you know, like I was saying, I've been out of work now for a few months and I guess I'm **pretty demoralized.**

Bruce: I hate being out of work. It's a real **blow** to the **old** self confidence.

Andy: Yeah, and it's really hard to pay the bills.

Bruce: What kind of work are you looking for?

Andy: I want to make a **career change** and get out of **journalism.** I've been trying to get into teaching or textbook writing. The problem is, however, I have very little experience in education.

Bruce: I remember that you used to write for the school newspaper. Journalism was always a **love** of yours. What made you want to **quit** journalism?

Andy: I guess I just **burned out**. I began to stop caring about the work I was
           doing. I was working **lots of overtime**. I never got home before four
           in the morning. Sometimes I'd be rushing around rewriting some story on a
           sewage treatment **plant** wondering what I was doing with my life.

Bruce: So you quit your job.

Andy: No. The paper was experiencing financial difficulties and **laying people
           off**. I **volunteered** to be laid off.

Bruce: Why did you do a thing like that?

Andy: Well, as I said, I was demoralized. Because of the financial **mess** and
           general mismanagement the **morale** at the paper was low.   They said they
           were going to cut **personnel** in the editorial department by 20% and were
           offering severance **bonuses** to those who volunteered to leave. So I
           took the money and ran.

Bruce: And how has the **job hunt** been so far?

Andy: Well, I've been **pounding the pavement**.   And I've sent out a lot of
           resumes, looked through a lot of **help wanteds**, written a lot of letters
           and made a lot of phone calls, but nothing has **panned out** yet.

Bruce: Have you had any **interviews** yet?

Andy: **A couple.** I'm still waiting to hear from them though.

Bruce: Is there anything I can do to help you out?

Andy: How would you feel if I used you as a **reference**?

Bruce: No problem. But remember, of course, I won't be back at my home address
           for another six weeks.

Andy: Right.

Bruce: I think teaching would be a very **rewarding field** to go into.

Andy: Yes, I think so, too. I've always liked working with kids. You have to go through a lot of **hassles** with the state **bureaucracy** before you can get a teaching **license,** however.

Bruce: (to the waiter) Can we have another **round?**

Andy: Let's get off this topic of my unemployment. How has your trip been so far?

DISCUSS

1. Losing a job can be a painful experience. Why might you lose your job? How could you get money when you are out of work? How do people feel and act when they are unemployed?

2. The **unemployment rate** in the U.S. was about 7% in 1989. What is it in your country? Who is the blame for unemployment? Because of **mergers** and acquisitions in the corporate world, many companies are undergoing personnel "restructuring" in which many people **are transferred,** laid off or **fired.** Is this **ethical?** Whose responsibility is job retraining?

3. It was **appropriate** that Bruce and Andy go to listen to blues music. Often the **lyrics** of blues songs are about being **down and out,** not having a job, not having any money, etc. Give Andy some advice so he won't be "singing the blues" for too much longer.

4. Computer programmers are in high demand; **tailors** have a hard time finding work. What are the jobs that are becoming more popular? What are jobs that are **diminishing** in popularity? What were your great grandfathers' occupations? What is your father's occupation?

5. New Orleans and Louisiana have a distinctive culture which has French, Spanish, Native American and African influences. The cuisine of the region, called Cajun, **incorporates** all these influences and is extremely **spicy.** What is Cajun food like? What are other spicy or hot cuisines? What are some **dishes?** Do you like them?

WRITE

Write a resume in English to get a job in the United States. You can either use your actual job experiences or make them up.

ACTIVE VOCABULARY REVIEW

The words are in alphabetical order. The definitions are scrambled in each group. AS A GLOSSARY to understand the lesson, find the word alphabetically and select the definition that fits the context. AS AN EXERCISE, write the correct word next to each definition. To save time, you can do the exercise orally in class and then write it as homework.

amateur _____ apartment

appropriate _____ not professional

apt. _____ four-year college degree

bachelor of arts, of science _____ a hard hit

blow [n] _____ proper; suitable

boatswain _____ government employees

bonus _____ lose interest from overwork

bureaucracy _____ profession or occupation

to burn out _____ ship foreman, not an officer

career _____ extra pay

career change _____ written material

cargo _____ emphasis

clips _____ a move from one career to another

concentration _____ contents of a ship

copy _____ a journalist's articles

copy editor _____ ship maintenance, docking, etc.

a couple _____ with honors

cum laude _____ time for completion

deadline _____ two, a few

deck department _____ one who edits articles, etc.

demoralized _____ to decrease

to diminish _____ particular kinds of food

dishes _____ discouraged, depressed

double scotch _____ without hope

down and out _____ twice the normal amount of whiskey

draft beer	_____	to improve a written document
to edit	_____	normally correct; fair; just
ethical	_____	to end an employee's job
field	_____	beer from a barrel
to fire	_____	area of knowledge or work
freighter	_____	title of a newspaper article
great-grandfather	_____	ship with cargo, not for passengers
hassle	_____	classified newspaper ads listing jobs
headlines	_____	grandfather's father
help wanteds	_____	problem; confusion
high-pressure	_____	to include, put together
to hire	_____	stressful, difficult
to incorporate	_____	to look for employment
interview	_____	to employ initially
job hunt	_____	a meeting to answer questions
journalist	_____	affection
to lay people off	_____	certificate indicating legal permission
license	_____	to terminate the employment
lots of	_____	a newspaper writer
love [n]	_____	much
lyrics	_____	area of concentration
major	_____	written text before publication
manuscript	_____	the words of a song
mergers and acquisitions	_____	confused situation
mess	_____	the buying and combining of companies
morale	_____	additional hours at work
occupation	_____	valued
old [adj., slang]	_____	distribution of the parts of a page
overtime	_____	job
page layout	_____	feeling of well-being
to pan out [informal]	_____	employees of a company
personnel	_____	text below a photo
photo	_____	a factory
photo captions	_____	to result
plant	_____	photograph

port	_____	to stop and leave
to pound	_____	to check for mistakes
pretty	_____	to walk to places to find a job
to proofread	_____	place for ship
to quit	_____	somewhat
recipient	_____	one who receives something
reference	_____	paper with your job history
resume	_____	giving satisfaction
rewarding	_____	difficult period
rough time	_____	one who knows about you
round	_____	hot-tasting
seaman	_____	a drink for each person
sewage	_____	street
spicy	_____	waste that goes down the drain
St. [abbreviation]	_____	sailor on a ship
staff	_____	turn in
submit	_____	to oversee or direct
supervise	_____	one who makes or fixes clothes
tailor	_____	to complete a deal quickly and leave
to take the money and run	_____	employees
tanker	_____	to be moved to a different location
to be transferred	_____	a teacher who teaches one student
tutor	_____	ship which transports petroleum
unemployment rate	_____	to work without pay; to offer willingly
to volunteer	_____	percent of people without work

Although the day is gray and damp, Dan and Shirley are taking a walk together. They talk about Shirley's career plans.

Dan: So, I hear that you're determined to start your own business.

Shirley: Yes. I'm planning on running a small private day-care service out of the house. It will be difficult at first, I know, but I'm going to give it a try anyway.

Dan: You've got lots of experience with children; nevertheless, a new business is a challenge to anyone. Were you unhappy working at the kindergarten? Is that why you're leaving?

Shirley: No. I was quite content at the kindergarten, but I've wanted to open my own day-care for awhile now. I'm glad I made the decision to leave even though they offered me a raise in salary. A day-care would fill a need in my neighborhood.

Dan: You left although they offered you a higher salary! You must really be determined.

Shirley: Yes, I am. And I'm willing to take the risk despite the financial setbacks. I had to take out a loan even though the interest was high.

Dan: Don't worry. I have a feeling your school will be a success. You have a way with children and even though you don't have any business experience, I think you'll be able to handle it.

Shirley: Well, thank you Dan, for your vote of confidence. Maybe I should hire you as my PR man.

ADVERBIAL CLAUSES OF CONCESSION AND THE USE OF SUBORDINATING CONJUNCTIONS

Although the day is gray and damp, Dan and Shirley are taking a walk together.
I had to take out a loan *even though the interest was high.*
I'm willing to take the risk *despite the financial setbacks.*
You've got lots of experience with children; *nevertheless, a new business is a challenge to anyone.*

REVIEW

In complex sentences, subordinating conjunctions such as *although, even though* and *though* are used to introduce an adverbial clause of concession which presents an idea that seems to conflict with the idea in the main clause
e.g.   *Though Andy had looked through a lot of help wanteds, written a lot of letters and made a lot of phone calls,* he hadn't been able to find a job.

The words *in spite of* and *despite* do the same job of introducing a clause of concession, but since they are prepositions they act in a different way. *In spite of* and *despite* come before a noun or a noun phrase.
e.g.   I went ice-skating *even though the temperatures were low.*
        I went ice-skating *in spite of the low temperatures.*
        I went ice-skating *despite the low temperatures.*

84

VOCABULARY VARIATIONS

I'm planning on running a small day-care service out of the house.
I'm planning to operate a small day-care service from the house.
I'm planning on opening a small day-care service at home.

I'm going to take the risk despite the financial setbacks.
I'm going to take a chance in spite of the financial drawbacks.
I'm going to take the plunge despite the financial risks.

I had to take out a loan.
I had to ask for a loan.
I had to borrow from the bank.

You have a way with children.
You have a talent for dealing with children.
You have a special ability to handle children.

PRACTICE

A. Fill in an appropriate subordinating conjunction based on the type of clause that follows the main clause. Pick from: *although, but...anyway, despite, though, even though.*
e.g. Andy wants to get into teaching *although* he has very little experience in education.

1.   Attempting to change fields in mid-career can be quite risky _____
      many professionals find it necessary.

2.   _____ journalism and textbook writing are distinct fields, they
      require similar skills.

3.   Kathy's business is progressing smoothly _____ some initial
      setbacks.

4.   We advised her not to take such a huge risk _____ she did it
      _____.

5.   Some experts predict that the U.S. will retain its economic strength into the
      twenty-first century _____ Japan is more advanced in the area of
      high technology.

85

6.   _____ her lack of experience, Mary has been given an excellent position.

7.   The bank approved the loan _____ he had a bad credit rating.

8.   _____ we had not offered to help him, Peter expected us to pay for his tuition.

9.   _____ our neighbors never complain, we knew that they are disturbed by the noisy parties that we throw from time to time.

10.   We seldom picnic on weekdays _____ we know our children enjoy it a lot.

B. Rewrite the following sentences so that you can use *despite* or *in spite of.*
e.g. Ronald Reagan was a very popular president *despite* his many errors.

1.   Hiro is thinking of a career change although he loves journalism.
    _____
    _____

2.   Ralph was laid off from his job at the shipping company even though he had given six years of service. _____
    _____

3.   We finished editing the manuscript on time even though the deadline was ridiculous._____
    _____

4.   Although there were recent paycuts, workers' morale at the auto plant remains high. _____
    _____

5.   Wayne dislikes spicy food; nevertheless, he's meeting his old staff at a cajun restaurant for lunch. _____
    _____

6.	Although the student felt very sick, she never failed to do her homework.
	_____
	_____

7.	They managed to get to the theater on time even though the traffic was heavy.
	_____
	_____

8.	Many people enjoy outdoor games in the winter although it is bitterly cold.
	_____
	_____

9.	Even though he was not formally educated, our friend became a millionaire.
	_____
	_____

10.	The children went skating on the thin ice although their parents had warned them
	against it. _____
	_____

C. Complete the sentences by adding either a main clause or a concession clause of your own.   e.g. Sachico doesn't want to be a commercial artist *although she is very talented.*

	Even though Bill's resume was very impressive, *his former supervisor did not recommend him highly.*

1.	Andy worked on tankers and freighters for three years	_____
	_____

2.	John is the recipient of many academic awards	_____
	_____

3.	Although being out of work can be demoralizing,	_____
	_____

4.	Despite the rough time Andy's been having,	_____
	_____

87

5. _____ even
    though I have a way with children.

6. Despite the high rent in the big cities _____
    _____

7. _____ now she
    is feeling very well and has taken up skiing.

8. Even though they have very little free time, _____
    _____

9. In spite of the many hardships that he encountered, _____
    _____

10. Although the students have been studying for only six months, _____
    _____

On a Steamboat up the Mississippi River from New Orleans to St. Louis

J. DE PRADO 1991.

Unit 7

ST. LOUIS
On a Steamboat up the Mississippi River

Noise proves nothing. Often a hen who has merely laid an egg cackles as if she had laid an asteroid.

We should be careful to get out of an experience only the wisdom that is in it--and stop there; lest we be like the cat that sits down on a hot stove-lid. She will never sit down on a hot stove-lid again, and that is well; but also she will never sit down on a cold one any more.

The old saw says, "Let a sleeping dog lie." Right. Still, when there is much at stake it is better to get a newspaper to do it.

Truth is the most valuable thing we have. Let us economize it.

It could probably be shown by facts and figures that there is no distinctly native American criminal class exept Congress.

The Autocrat of Russia possesses more power than any other man in the earth, but he cannot stop a sneeze.

I have traveled more that anyone else and I have noticed that even the angels speak English with an **accent.**

NARRATIVE

After several days spent with Bruce, Andy is feeling much better. Bruce has **cheered him up,** made him laugh and now Andy is **back on track** and feeling confident about his **prospects** of finding a job. Their time together must **come to a close,** however, because Bruce's next adventure is about to begin.

Bruce will travel from New Orleans up the Mississippi River to St. Louis aboard the steamboat, **Delta** Queen. **Accompanying him** will be his friend from college, Anita Hollingsworth. Anita, a **native** of St. Louis, has taken this trip before and was the one who recommended it to Bruce. The **Delta Queen** is a **restored paddlewheel steamboat,** just like the kind that used **to ply** the great rivers in the nineteenth century. Although it would be much quicker to fly, drive or take a train, taking a leisurely trip on a paddlewheel steamboat offers a glimpse into America's past. In addition, the trip affords Bruce and Anita plenty of time to talk and meet new friends.

DIALOGUE

Bruce and Anita are relaxing out on the upper deck of the steamboat several hours after their departure from New Orleans.

92

Bruce: Look at that **sunset!**

Anita: It's beautiful, isn'it?

Bruce: The sky is so orange . . . It makes the water look almost as if it's on fire.

Anita: Watching the sun set over the water seems to make it twice as spectacular.

Bruce: I think there's something very **soothing** about looking out over a large **body of water.**

Anita: Yes, it is peaceful, but for me it's also exciting. I try to imagine what lies around the **bend** or on the distant shore. Rivers and oceans seem to invite adventure. Whenever I'm on a boat on the Mississippi, I can't help but think I'm on some grand expedition, like Huckleberry Finn.

Bruce: You know, I read *Huckleberry Finn* a long time ago, but I can't remember the **plot.**

Anita: It's the **tale** of a young boy, Huck, who travels down the Mississippi. He starts the trip with his **brutish,** drunken father, escapes from his father and then continues the trip with a **runaway slave** named Jim. They have good times and **close calls** as they float past the towns and cities of middle America. They meet up with all sorts of **con men** and **hustlers.**

Bruce: Yes, that's really a great story. What I remember most about the story was the remarkable use of **dialects.** Twain knew the **everyday** English of **dozens** of regions and could therefore **instill** in his characters authentic colloquial speech. He seemed to have a real **ear** for the language.

Anita: That's what makes a good writer, the ability to pick up idioms and phrases of speech **overheard** in conversation and then **incorporate** them into one's writing.

Bruce: It's more than just idioms. Twain was able to **duplicate** the accents and phrases of a **host** of different kinds of people. The ability to master dialects is, in fact, a very important aspect of my own craft of acting. If, for example, you **land the part** of and Irishman or a **cowboy** from Texas in a play, you had better be able to speak like one.

Anita: I see what you are saying. I think it's really hard to speak consistently with an accent. When I try to speak with and Australian accent, for example, it sounds really bad.

Bruce: Well, Anita, you seem to speak pretty consistently in a Southern accent.

Anita: There you go again! People at Georgetown always used to **tease** me about my accent. I used to tell them that my English was perfect and that they had a Northern accent.

Bruce: I didn't mean to give you a hard time. I guess everybody has an accent.

Anita: Right. Hey, I thought you said you didn't know much about Mark Twain.

Bruce: Well, I don't really. I have a friend who is an actor and **stand-up comedian** and he **goes on and on** about how great Mark Twain was.

Anita: I guess you could say Twain is the **grandfather** of American comedy. He was **tireless** in his **castigation** of America. Government, morality, manners: none were safe from his **barbed tongue.**

Bruce: Yes, to me what makes good **satire,** whether it's a **political cartoon** or someone talking on a **late night talk show,** is the ability to **tweak** the nose of those in power.

Anita :   Hey, are you getting cold?

Bruce: Yeah, a little.

Anita: What do you say we **go below** and get a cup of coffee.

Bruce: Sounds good to me.

DISCUSS

1. What makes something funny? What are some **jokes** from your country? What are some American jokes you've heard?

2. Most people think that they speak their **native** language without an accent. Are there different accents in your language? What are they? Is there a "correct" accent for speaking English? If so, what is it?

3. Although travel by airplane is much faster, many people enjoy taking ferries or boats. What are some ferries or boats that you've been on? Where did you **embark?** What was your destination? What are the advantages and disadvantages of traveling by ferry or boat?

4. Bruce and Anita seem to get along pretty well. Neither of them is married. What do you think? Should Bruce get married? Should he get married to Anita? What about Anita? Should she fall in love with a guy like Bruce? Knowing what you already know about Bruce, what advice or information would you give Anita if you could have a nice private talk with her?

5. Is it all right to **mock** and **poke fun** at those in power? Do you have the right to **level biting criticism** and **satirize** polilticians, **prominent** business people, entertainers, etc.? Or should they be respected and not **subject** to **demeaning** jokes?

WRITE

Write a humorous story of 125 words. You can transcribe a joke, write a satire of someone or something, or write about a funny thing you have seen or experienced. It can be true or **made up.**

ACTIVE VOCABULARY REVIEW

The words are in alphabetical order in groups of five and the meanings are scrambled within each group. Find the word alphabetically and select the meaning that fits the context. As a review exercise, write the correct word next to its definition. You can do the exercise orally in class and then write it as homework.

accent_____ a return to normal functioning

to accompany_____ ability to criticize

back on track_____ place where a river turns

barbed tongue_____ distinguishing manner of pronunciation

bend _____ to go with

biting _____ e.g. lake, river, ocean, sea, etc.

body of water_____ to scold publicly

brutish _____ sarcastic

to castigate _____ to make someone happy

to cheer up _____ savage, stupid, mean

close call_____ a horseman on a ranch

to come to a close _____ triangular branching end of a river

con man _____ to end

cowboy _____ a near accident

delta _____ a confidence man who deceives to steal

Delta Queen _____ degrading, humbling

demeaning _____ typical language of a region

dialect _____ twelve

dozen _____ to repeat, make another

to duplicate _____ name of the river boat

ear_____ to talk for too long

to embark_____ to go down from the deck to the inside

everyday _____ to get on a plane, boat, etc.

to go below _____ common

to go on and on _____ ability to imitate voices, dialects, etc.

96

grandfather	con man, one who gets what he wants
host	to put in
hustler	include
to incorporate	a great number
to instill	founder, leading figure

Irishman	any funny thing
joke	someone from Ireland
to land the part	TV program in which guests appear
late night talk show	to criticize
to level criticism	to get a role in a play

to make up	from birth
to mock	a person born in that place
native [noun]	imitate in fun or derision
native [adjective]	to hear the conversation of others
to overhear	to create in one's imagination

paddlewheel steamboat	to sail back and forth
plot	19th century river boat
to ply	humorous drawing of a person or issue
to poke fun	the essential events in a story
political cartoon	to ridicule lightly

prominent	chances
prospects	a slave who has escaped from the master
restored	ridicule, sarcasm, to attack evil
runaway slave	famous
satire	cleaned and repaired to look like new

to satirize	tells jokes in front of an audience
slave	exposed
to soothe	a person owned by another person
stand-up comedian	to attack with satire
subject	to calm by gentleness and flattery

sunset	_____	to give a twisting pinch
tale	_____	does not become tired
to tease	_____	story
tireless	_____	the sun going down below the horizon
to tweak	_____	friendly mocking, poking fun

SPEAK

Julie is talking to her roommate Beatriz, who is a visiting student from Brazil.

Julie: What's the matter, Beatriz? You look so depressed? Are you suffering from Blue Monday Syndrome?

Beatriz: I'm just really frustrated. In my English class today we spent the whole period on pronunciation. I'll never learn to speak English like a native!

Julie: I thought your school's policy was to spend every Friday in the language lab doing pronunciation exercises.

Beatriz: It is. But it was the teacher's decision to concentrate on pronunciation today. It was really difficult because we all have such different accents. And my accent is the worst of all.

Julie: Beatriz, that's not true. You do have an accent, but it's not that strong. Besides, many prominent people in the United States have foreign accents. It's not a measure of your intelligence, you know.

Beatriz: You're crazy! Americans speak with an American accent.

Julie: That's true of most people who were born here. But there are many people who become naturalized American citizens who retain their foreign accents. For example, Henry Kissinger's accent is still very strong, and he was one of the most prominent men in the country's political history.

Beatriz: Maybe you're right. But I still don't think my accent will ever disappear.

Julie: Oh, cheer up. Maybe it won't disappear completely, but it will certainly improve if you speak English as much as possible. In a few years' time you'll probably be speaking almost like a native.

Beatriz: I try to speak English a lot. But part of my problem is that I'm afraid to talk to Americans. I know they'll poke fun at me.

Julie: You're talking to me, aren't you?

Beatriz: Yes, but I know you. I'm not afraid of you.

Julie: Aha! If that's the case, doesn't it stand to reason that if you talk to more Americans, you'll get to know more Americans? Then you won't be afraid any more.

Beatriz: As usual, the logic of your argument is perfect. Someday I'll be able to argue with you -- in English!

Henry Kissinger's accent is still very strong.

In a *few years' time* you'll probably be speaking almost like a native.

Part of my problem is that I'm afraid to talk to most Americans.

As usual, the *logic of your argument* is perfect.

REVIEW

The possessive form of a noun is generally constructed in one of two ways: by adding *'s* or *'* to the noun, or by a prepositional phrase with *of*.

In general, *'s* and *'* are used for persons (John's car) and living beings (dog's tail) and geographical (New York's skyline) and time nouns (today's paper). The *of*-construction is used with inanimate objects.

e.g. Peter's mother lives in Paris.

The cat's fur was long and silky.

London's parks are famous.

This week's news is very interesting.

The color of the lake was dark blue.

To form the possessive, add *'s* to any animate noun in the singular, or to an irregular plural not ending in "s" (e.g. children). With regular plurals ending in "s", merely add *'*.

e.g. The men's lockers were at the far end of the building.

Our friends' cars were parked in front of the house.

VOCABULARY VARIATIONS

I'm really [frustrated!
[irritated!
[annoyed!

You look [depressed.
[sad.
[upset.
[down in the dumps.

100

I don't think   [my accent will ever disappear.

                [my accent will ever go away.

                [I'll ever lose my accent.

                [I'll ever get rid of my accent.

PRACTICE

A. Place the phrase in Italics into the appropriate category.

    Example: Where is *yesterday's paper?*

                    (time noun)

1. She didn't give it *a moment's thought.*
2. There is an enormous tree in *the center of the park.*
3. Ben lives in *California's most liberal district.*
4. She spends *the majority of her time reading novels.*
5. *My cousin's wedding* is on June 24.
6. *The crew's aim* was to save the ship.
7. The explorer was amazed at *the bear's long, sharp claws.*
8. *The curriculum of this school* does not meet my needs.
9. Have you read *this week's magazines?*
10. *The strategy of the employers* was to avoid a confrontation with the workers.

B. Fill the blanks with an appropriate possessive noun or *of*-construction.

1. The _____ mother slept restlessly while waiting for him to come home.
2. Sandra abhors the _____ onions.
3. _____ new girlfriend is very amusing.
4. I love to listen to the _____ waves at the beach.
5. He won't take a leave of absence because he can't afford to miss _____ pay.
6. Venice is one of _____ most beautiful cities.
7. _____ newspapers give details of another catastrophic oil spill.
8. In a few _____ time it will be warm again.
9. The news _____ in the election took everybody by surprise.
10. The _____ policy is to attract new customers by advertising on T.V.

C. Using your own vocabulary, complete the following sentences.

1.   The hem of

2.   I borrowed Frank's

3.   She hates to use her little brother's

4.   Some of Tokyo's

5.   The shade of

6.   The intensity of

7.   Macy's department store is

8.   The roof of the bus was

9.   St. Paul's church in London is

10.   The end of the movie was

The World of Business

Unit 8

HOUSTON
The World of Business

PROSPECTUS   **September 1, 1989**
Dreyfus Worldwide Dollar Money Market Fund, Inc.

Dreyfus Worldwide Dollar Money Market Fund, Inc. (the "Fund") is an open-end, **diversified**, management investment company, known as a money market **mutual fund**. Its goal is to provide you with as high a level of current **income** as is consistent with the preservation of capital and the maintenance of **liquidity**.

The Fund seeks to maintain a stabilized price of $1 per share. You can invest, reinvest or **redeem shares** at any time without charge or **penalty**.

The Fund provides free redemption checks, which you can use in amounts of $500 or more for cash or to pay bills. You continue to earn income on the amount of the check until it clears. You can purchase or redeem shares readily by telephone using Dreyfus *TeleTransfer*.

The Dreyfus Corporation professionally manages the Fund's **portfolio**.

This **Prospectus** sets forth concisely information about the Fund that you should know before investing. It should be read and retained for future reference.

Part B (also known as the Statement of Additional Information), dated September 1, 1989, which may be revised from time to time, provides a further discussion of certain areas in this Prospectus and other matters which may be of interest to some investors. It has been filed with the **Securities and Exchange Commission** and is incorporated **herein** by reference. For a free copy, write to the address or call one of the telephone numbers listed under "General Information" in this Prospectus. When telephoning, ask for Operator 665.

TABLE OF CONTENTS

THESE **SECURITIES** HAVE NOT BEEN APPROVED OR DIS-APPROVED BY THE SECURITIES AND EXCHANGE COMMISSION OR ANY STATE SECURITIES COMMISSION NOR HAS THE SECURITIES AND EXCHANGE COMMISSION OR ANY STATE SECURITIES COMMISSION PASSED UPON THE ACCURACY OR **ADEQUACY** OF THIS PROSPECTUS. ANY REPRESENTATION TO THE CONTRARY IS A CRIMINAL OFFENSE.

NARRATIVE

Al Karakis has invited Bruce to spend a few days at his **palatial** Houston home. Al is the son of a wealthy Greek shipping **magnate**. He has **struck off** on his own in the business world and has done very well. He made his first million in oil. But when prices **slumped**, he got out of the oil business and into compact disc manufacturing. Al was getting his M.B.A. while Bruce was an undergraduate at Georgetown. The two met on a golf course in Northern Virginia and struck up a friendship. In the **intervening** years, Al has kept up his passion for golf; Bruce hasn't played since college. Today they're playing 18 holes **for old time's sake**.

DIALOGUE

Bruce: Remember back in our school days when we used to walk the course and carry our golf bags?

Al: Yes, but you sweat a lot less with these golf carts.

Bruce: You save time, too.

Al: That's the most important thing. You know what they say, "Time is money."

Bruce: Yes. You've obviously managed your time well, judging by your financial success. How did you manage to take time off to golf?

Al: Being relaxed and **level-headed** is key to big financial decisions.

Bruce: I think the ability to relax and stay cool is essential in all professions: All audiences can detect a nervous actor.

Al: That's for sure. I used to carry a **beeper** with me when I golfed, but then I'd always get calls in the middle of a game.

Bruce: I can see how that would **mess up** your stroke.

Al: Now I just wait 'till I get back to the office. I'm refreshed and I can **tackle** all the phone calls and **faxes** I received when I was out.

Bruce: Life is really fast-paced these days for you, what with all your faxes and beepers.

Al: What about you? Didn't you tell me you regularly fly on the Concorde?

Bruce: I guess I'm caught up in the **rat race**, too. I do enjoy the convenience of a short flight from London to New York.

Al: I agree. It's worth the extra money.

Bruce: How have you made all this money of yours, Al, if you don't mind my being so **nosy**?

Al: I keep no secrets from you, buddy! Well, first I **fancied** myself an oil **tycoon**, but then **the bottom dropped out of that market**.

Bruce: So what did you do?

Al: I took my profits and started a company that manufactures compact discs.

Bruce: I thought they were all made in Japan.

Al: That's just the problem. We don't manufacture enough in this country anymore.

Bruce: I guess that accounts for our **gaping** trade deficit.

Al: Yes. An economy which doesn't make things is **unsound** to the **core**.

Bruce: Here we are at the first hole. Remember, Al: Relax.

DISCUSS

1. Japan's "bullet train" is the fastest in the world. Both Al and Bruce are regular travelers on it. What are some other fast trains? Why take a fast train when you can take a plane? Is it necessary to travel so fast?

2. Al is a golf fanatic. Many young people, however, are bored by golf. How is golf played? What is its attraction?

3. What is a budget deficit? a trade deficit? How can you **get rid of** them?

4. In 1992 the European Economic Community (EEC) will enter the world market as a force. These European countries will have a common **currency**. They will reduce trade barriers among themselves. Why are they doing this? How do you think it will affect the international economic situation?

5. Al is extremely wealthy. Is it good to be rich? Are all rich people happy? What are some problems which might be caused by being rich?

WRITE

In a **fit** of generosity, Al sends you a check for US$ 100,000. In a 125-word essay, describe how you would spend it.

ACTIVE VOCABULARY REVIEW

The words are in alphabetical order. The definitions are scrambled in each group. AS A GLOSSARY to understand the lesson, find the word alphabetically and select the definition that fits the context. AS AN EXERCISE, write the correct word next to each definition. To save time, you can do the exercise orally in class and then write it as homework.

adequacy: _____ yearly
annual: _____ instrument to signal a telephone call
banquet: _____ appropriateness
beeper:_____ a shortened version
condensed:_____ an elaborate meal

core:_____ to imagine (oneself)
currency:_____ payment from company profits
to diversify:_____ money
dividend:_____ the heart, center
to fancy:_____ to divide your investment in various stocks

fax: _____ in memory of past experiences
fit: _____ to remove
for old time's sake:_____ wide difference
gaping: _____ machine that transmits documents
to get rid of:_____ sudden impulse

glut: _____ money earned
herein:_____ calm, rational
income:_____ coming between
intervening:_____ in something mentioned before
level-headed:_____ excessive supply

liquidity:_____ a very influential person
magnate:_____ to interfere with
to mess up: _____ easily converted into cash
mutual fund: _____ inquisitive, curious
nosy: _____ one in which the investors are co-owners

110

palatial:_____ the main points of a stock

penalty:_____ a list of an investor's securities

portfolio:_____ a fast pace of life

prospectus:_____ a fine imposed because of an offense

rat race [informal]:_____ like a palace

to redeem:_____ agency that controls the stock market

securities:_____ a unit of the capital of a company

Securities & Exchange Commission:_____ to decline temporarily

share:_____ to convert stocks into cash

to slump:_____ stocks, bonds

struck off [verb: to strike off]:_____ a sharp decline in the value of stock

to tackle:_____ to move independently

the bottom dropped out of the market:_____ unstable

tycoon:_____ to attack

unsound:_____ a powerful industrialist

SPEAK

After work, Claire, Rose and James have gotten together at a cafe to relax a little.

James: Rose, you didn't show up, *so* we went ahead and ordered some beer. Why are you late? Is everything okay?

Rose: Yes, everything's fine. I just had a tough time at work, *so* it was hard for me to get away on time.

Claire: How bad was it?

Rose: Mr. Whitehaven was out of the office for most of the month. *Therefore*, he hadn't turned in any of his work until this week.

James: How much work did he give you?

Rose: He brought in some new figures *in order to* have them incorporated into this month's financial report.

James: He wants the new figures to be added to this report?

111

Rose: Yeah.

Claire: I'm so sorry. Not completing this month's report means that next month you'll
           be doing both this report and the annual report together.

James: Not only that, but adding those figures to the report at this late date results in it
           not being finished for the speech at the **banquet** dinner *either*.

Rose: I know, I am going to have a heavy workload in the coming weeks. Peter,
           can you pour me a beer? How has your day been?

CLAUSES OF RESULT AND PURPOSE

Rose, you didn't show up, *so* we went ahead and ordered some beer.

He brought in some new figures *in order to* have them incorporated into this month's
financial report.

112

The words *so, therefore, thus,* and *consequently* are used to show **result**.

However, they are not used in the same way.

e.g.   The bus didn't come, *so* we walked to school.

Sales kept dropping off; *therefore,* they went out of business.

Their plans fell through; *thus,* they never attained their goals.

John had never been to Paris before; *consequently,* he got lost.

The words *in order to, so that,* and *for the purpose of* are used to show **purpose**.

e.g.   He has two jobs *in order to* pay his mortgage.

They climbed to the top of the mountain *so that* they could see the beautiful sight.

They have come to the United States *for the purpose of* signing a trade agreement.

VOCABULARY VARIATIONS

At this late date...
At this late stage...
At the eleventh hour...
At the last minute...

In the coming weeks...
In the next few weeks...
In the weeks ahead...

How bad was it?
How serious was it?
How difficult was it?

PRACTICE

A. Punctuate the following sentences. Capitalize letters where necessary.

1.   The deadline is in one week therefore we have to work overtime.

2.   There was an oil **glut** recently consequently gasoline prices were lower.

3.   OPEC was formed to protect oil-producing member countries.

4.   Rose was overworked thus meeting with her friends was a good idea.

5.   I'm going to a banquet dinner on Friday so I need to have the dress by Thursday.

6.   The child fell sick consequently they put off the trip.

7.   We don't enjoy hiking so we'll rent a car.

8.   He never pays back his debts to his friends therefore they never lend him money.

9.   There was not enough time to take in the museums thus we decided to extend our stay in New York for another day.

10. The house was too small for such a large family the father bought a new one therefore.

B. Complete the following sentences with ideas of your own.

1.   Trade blocks have been formed in order to _____
     _____.

2.   Diana is going to leave Houston so that _____
     _____.

3.   Larry loves Italian food. Therefore,
     _____
     _____.

4.   Our company has started to manufacture both children's clothing and sportswear for the purpose of _____
     _____.

5.   The weather was absolutely awful so _____
     _____.

6.   We got tired of cooking. Consequently,
     _____

7.   They are studying computer science for the purpose of _____
_____.

8.   We waited in line in order to _____
_____.

9.   Mary jogs every day; she, therefore, _____
_____.

10. They hadn't witnessed the accident so _____
_____.

C. Respond to the following questions. Use *in order to, so that, therefore, so,* and *for the purpose of.*

1.   Why are you studying English?

2.   Why should companies diversify?

3.   Why do companies need monthly and annual reports?

4.   Why do some people have to make a change in the middle of their careers?

5.   What is the purpose of labor unions?

6.   Why should students arrive on time every morning?

7.   Why does the judge ask so many questions?

8.   Why did the pianist practice every day?

9.   What is the purpose of insurance companies?

10. Why does man explore outer space?

A University Professor in Mexico City

Unit 9

MEXICO CITY
A University Professor

The Growth of Shanty Towns in the Third World

By the end of the century, the urban population of the third world will have increased 20-fold since 1920. The world level of urbanization--the percentage of people living in centers with more than 5,000 inhabitants--is rising steadily and will exceed 50 per cent by the year 2000. In the third world, **population growth** averages more than 2 per cent a year, while urban growth is twice as high and the growth of shanty towns four times higher. This series of doubles is now one of the main threats to the established order.

Rising urbanization is the result of two factors: the general decline in the proportion of the workforce employed in agriculture; the spontaneous (unplanned) concentration of industrial activity and services around a number of 'growth poles.' In the third world, urbanization is fueled by population pressure and rural poverty, which drives people to the towns even when there are no jobs there. To slow this rural exodus would require a deliberate policy of improving the peasants' living conditions, which is far from a priority in most third-world countries.

In 1981, the United Nations calculated that 800 million people were living in absolute poverty throughout the world, 600 million of them in the countryside. These latter are prime candidates for urban migration, for the towns offer them greater access to the social, hygienic and educational infrastructure, as well as the possibility of employment, even if marginal, in the **informal sector**. The lure of the modern city, symbol of progress, is often irresistible: third-world town-dwellers numbered 900 million in 1981 and will swell to 1,200 million by 1985. The constant spread of cities has everywhere turned certain districts into slums, resulting in ramshackle housing, neighborhoods of squatters and, above all, sizeable shanty towns.

The term 'shanty town' was first applied to conglomerations of irregular dwellings built of discarded materials. The process is quite uniform: rural poverty drives people into towns where modern housing is lacking; they build primitive shanties devoid of all comfort on land that is not their own and in terrible conditions. Few of these dwellings have water taps or electricity.

Shanty towns may be built of cardboard, but they are not 'cardboard towns.' An integral part of sprawling cities, they have their own social and ethnic divisions. Each shanty town has its 'rich' and 'poor,' and none is spared the ravages of property speculation.

NARRATIVE

Bruce's head spins as he winds his way in a cab through the notorious Mexico City traffic on his way from the airport to the university. Bruce ponders his condition. His shortness of breath could be caused by Mexico City's high altitude. Or it might be due to the thick smog that constantly hugs the city. Some of his lightheadedness comes from being in a foreign place, no doubt. He has been bombarded by a new language, new customs, and new laws. His senses reel from unfamiliar sights, sounds and smells. Bruce finds his condtion not altogether unpleasant, however. There is an exhilaration that all of this newness inspires. And so, despite his wheezing and slight nausea, Bruce finds himself smiling and his adrenalin rushing as he is bounced around in the back seat of the cab as it careens around corners and snakes through traffic.

Bruce's destination is the Social Sciences Building at the university, where he will visit his friend, Peter Van Winkle. Peter is a newly-appointed professor of sociology here.

Bruce: Hola, Pedro. Que pasa, amigo? [Translation: Hello, Peter. What's happening friend?]

Peter: Hey, Bruce. It's great to see you. You're looking good. And your Spanish isn't too bad, either.

Bruce: I'm afraid I don't remember too much of the Spanish that I learned in high school, but I'd like to brush up on it while I'm here. But for now let's speak English, O.K.? We have so many stories to tell each other and so much catching up to do that I'm afraid we won't get very far if we speak Spanish.

Peter: Fine. What do you say we leave this cramped office and walk across campus to a cafe?

Bruce: Lead the way. So you look very professorial. It's hard to believe that my peers are already established academics.

Peter: (laughing) Well, I'm not exactly established. I don't even have tenure yet.

Bruce: But you have published some books, haven't you?

Peter: Yes. In fact, I've just had a book published that was fairly well-received.

Bruce: Congratulations! I'll have to take you out to dinner one night to celebrate ...
           Say, those murals are awesome. Who did them?

Peter: Those are Diego Rivera's murals.

Bruce: They're magnificent. So big and bold.

Peter: Are you familiar with Rivera at all?

Bruce: I'm afraid not. Who was he?

Peter: He was a socialist and one of the most popular artists in Mexican history.

Bruce: It seems that much of the art of Latin America is tied up with politics. Why do
           you think that is so?

Peter: Well, here the disparity between the rich and the poor is great. The class
           struggle, as the Marxists would say, is intense.

Bruce: Rivera depicts workers and peasants in his mural as strong and determined. He
           paints them with, it seems, a certain compassion and affection.

Peter: Yes, that's because he was a partisan on the side of their struggle against
           oppression. Most artists in Latin America--painters, writers, poets, whatever--
           in some way address the grinding poverty that we face here South of the
           Border.

Bruce: And you, Peter, have you turned into a socialist?

Peter: When it comes to politics, Bruce, I don't like wearing a label. What I do know
           is that in my sociological studies of Mexico and its people I see a crying need
           for reform.

Bruce: What do you mean?

Peter: Well, in this country, like most others in the Third World, infant mortality, illiteracy, malnutrition, and disease are rampant. These conditions are greatly intensified in our ever-burgeoning shanty towns. Something needs to be done.

Bruce: I guess you're right on that score. But what?

Peter: I don't know, I'm only a sociologist; I only study the problems. I leave their solutions to the politicians.

DISCUSS

1. Mexico City suffers from some of the worst air pollution in the world. This problem is by no means limited to the Third World, however. Los Angeles and, to a lesser extent, Tokyo are also victims of smog. The environment and its pollution are on many people's minds today. Why do we have urban air pollution? What are the costs of letting air pollution continue? What would be the costs of trying to clean it up?

2. Who is to blame for shanty towns?

3. Socialism has had its proponents and opponents for many years now. Divide the class in half. Have one half offer arguments in favor of socialism; let the other half argue against it.

4. Peter says that most art in Latin America is political. Is this true? Do art and politics mix? Should all art be political? Should any art be political?

5. Mexico's economy is in bad shape. Part of the problem is Mexico's massive debts. If the government wants to pay the debts back it has to raise hard currency by increasing productivity and imposing austerity measures. Taking this course, however, could mean strikes and labor unrest. What caused Mexico's debt? Should the debts be paid back? How? What's a long-term solution for Mexico's economic woes?

WRITE

All countries suffer from social ills. In a 150-word essay describe a problem in your society. Offer a possible solution.

121

ACTIVE VOCABULARY REVIEW

The words are in alphabetical order. The definitions are scrambled in each group. AS A GLOSSARY to understand the lesson, find the word alphabetically and select the definition that fits the context. AS AN EXERCISE, write the correct word next to each definition. To save time, you can do the exercise orally in class and then write it as homework.

academic:_____	feelings of love
adrenalin:_____	a professor in a university
affection:_____	a heart-quickening hormone
altitude:_____	inspiring, respect and wonder
awesome:_____	height

to bombard:_____	hard paper material
to brush up on:_____	growing
burgeoning:_____	to lean sideways while moving
cardboard:_____	to revive an old skill
to careen:_____	to bomb

class struggle:_____	a strong need
compassion:_____	the fight between the rich and the poor
conglomeration:_____	the feeling of sympathy
cramped:_____	a group
crying need:_____	with little space

disparity:_____	pertaining to a specific culture and people
ethnic:_____	times as many or much: 10-fold
exodus:_____	to promote
-fold [suffix]:_____	a mass emigration
to fuel:_____	difference

to get far:_____	matters of sanitation
to have one's head spin:_____	to advance, to make progress
hygienic:_____	the inability to read
illiteracy:_____	death rate of babies before age one
infant mortality:_____	to be confused

informal sector:_____ strong, extremely active

infrastructure:_____ a sign, name-tag

integral:_____ water system, transportation, roads, etc.

intense:_____ important, inseparable, closely associated

label:_____ business not regulated by the government

lightheadedness:_____ the lack of healthy food

malnutition:_____ famous for being evil

mural:_____ unjust control of people and ideas

notorious:_____ a large painting on a wall

oppression:_____ dizziness

partisan:_____ persons of one's own status

peasants:_____ a strong supporter of a movement

peers:_____ not yet refined

primitive:_____ like a professor

professorial:_____ rural farmers under a landowner

ramshackle:_____ poor, run-down urban areas

to ravage:_____ to move in a confused manner

to reel:_____ smoke + fog, polluted air

slums:_____ to violently destroy

smog:_____ flimsy, poorly built

to snake:_____ dispersed over a large area

speculation:_____ one living in a place without permission

sprawling:_____ guessing in economic matters

squatter:_____ a permanent contract for a professor

tenure:_____ to move like a snake

tied up:_____ the same everywhere

uniform [adj.]:_____ to move in a crooked way

water tap:_____ favorably reviewed

well-received:_____ connected to

to wind:_____ faucet, water outlet

123

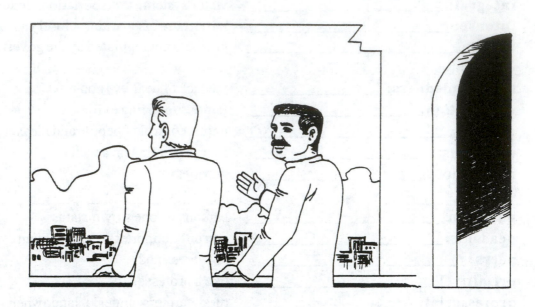

Bruce and Peter are at Peter's house catching up with each other's lives.

Bruce: This is really a nice set-up you've got here Peter.

Peter: Yes, the house was part of the terms of employment with the University.
           Most professors are given assistance with housing.

Bruce: Is that why you chose Mexico City over UCLA?   I know it can't be because of
           the quality of the air.

Peter: You're right, both Mexico City and Los Angeles have pretty bad smog.
           I chose Mexico City University because of the contract I was offered.
           They offered me not only a full-time faculty position for three years but also
           a fellowship that allows me to do research here in Mexico, during the
           summers.

Bruce: That sounds great. So your professional life is set; what about your social life?
           You must know some interesting people either romantically or socially.

Peter: Yes, I've met a lot of nice people here and I really should make more of an effort to see them.

Bruce: What do you mean?

Peter: Well, with all the work I've been doing, I've had neither the time nor the energy to pursue an active social life. But I plan to make up for it at least while you're here, so let's get moving.

PARALLEL STRUCTURE WITH PAIRED CONJUNCTIONS

You're right, *both* Mexico City *and* Los Angeles have pretty bad smog.

They offered me *not only* a full-time faculty position for three years *but also* a fellowship that allows me to do research here in Mexico during the summers.

You must know some interesting people, *either* romantically *or* socially.

With all the work I've been doing I've had *neither* the time *nor* energy to pursue an active social life.

REVIEW

The rules of parallel structure also apply when the conjunctions are paired as in *both...and, not only... but (also), either...or,* and *neither...nor.* In the *both...and* construction, the verb is always in the plural. With *not only...but (also), either...or* and *neither...nor,* the subject closest to the verb determines whether the verb is singular or plural.

e.g.   *Both* John *and* his wife are engineers.
        He is *not only* a famous architect *but also* an outstanding sculptor
        Choose *either* the bicycle *or* the roller skates.
        Neither the tourist *nor* the guide could speak the local dialect.
        Either you *or* your parents are to blame.

125

So your professional life is set.
So your professional life is all in order.
So your professional life is arranged.

Let's get moving.
Let's make a move.
Let's go.

They are catching up with each other's lives.
They are getting caught up on each other's lives.

PRACTICE

A. Combine the following sentences using any of the paired conjunctions that you find suitable: both...and, either...or, neither...nor, not only...but (also),
e.g.   Crying won't get you very far.   Shouting won't get you very far.
Neither crying nor shouting will get you very far.

1.   The children were awed by the sight of the tattooed man.
The children were repulsed by the sight of the tattooed man.

2.   He is studying the history of the country. He is also studying its current economic problems.

3.   They should not pay back the debt. They should not borrow any more money.

4.   Her shortness of breath was caused by the high altitude. It's also possible that her shortness of breath was caused by the smog.

5.   Charles' peers admired him for his compassion. Charles' patients admired him for his compassion.

6.   The student possibly wanted to study biology.
The student possibly wanted to study medicine.

7. The guests liked the room facing the sea.
    The guests liked the room facing the mountains.

8. They don't want to drive to California.
    They don't want to fly to California.

9. You must not smoke in the restaurant.
    You must not sing in the rstaurant.

10. He was hired because of his knowledge.
    He was hired because of his energetic, pleasant manner.

B. Find the errors in the following sentences and correct them.
e.g. Both tenure and being published are necessary for a professor to be secure in his
     position.
     Both having tenure and being published are necessary for a
     professor to be secure   in his position.

1. Both art and music is tied up with politics.

2. Neither the students nor their teacher were interested in the field trip.

3. Both sewing and to knit are hobbies of mine.

4. Not only politicians but journalists and also actors and artists affect public opinion.

5. I told him that we would have either an unclean environment or raise taxes.

6. He enjoys both playing tennis and also watching it.

7. Ann neither bought the book or borrowed it from the library.

8. The students are gifted not only in music and also in acting.

9. The player was either sick of playing nor too tired to play.

10. Either the mother or the father are at home in the afternoon.

C. Complete the following sentences with ideas of your own.

1. Neither _____ nor _____ harmful to the environment.

2. Not only _____ but also _____ are often manifested in art.

3. Both Guatemala and Costa Rica are _____

4. Not only education but also _____ necessary to eradicate the social ills of Third World countries.

5. Being in a foreign country can cause feelings of either _____ or _____.

6. The janitor promised to repair the _____ and the _____ _____ in the bathroom.

7. She neither _____ on the air conditioner, nor _____ the window when she entered the room.

8. The police officer told the driver that neither the _____ nor the _____ were on.

9. Both the _____ and the _____ agreed that the defendant was innocent.

10. We were not only _____ but also _____ to find a shelter for the night.

Exploring the Grand Canyon on Muleback

130

Unit 10

ARIZONA
Exploring the Grand Canyon on Muleback

BLUE JEANS GUIDE

U.S.A.

The American National Parks **deserve** their **reputation** if you are looking for beautiful **scenery**, you will be well and truly **satisfied**. When the frenzied pace of the cities begins to get you down, it really does you good to go and relax in the wide open spaces where every **slightest** sign of life is **preserved**.

GRAND CANYON NATIONAL PARK

If you can only see one park, it must be this one. You will not be **disappointed**. It is a **unique** sight and no photograph can ever **do it justice**. The sheer size of the canyon will **astound** you and its beauty will really make you think ... It is an **absolutely fantastic** place.

The South **Rim** is open all year and more interesting than the North Rim which is only open in summer. **Accommodation**: Naturally such a popular place is outrageously **commercialized**. Rooms in **bungalows** are very expensive. The three cheapest places to stay are: Yavapai Lodge, the Motor Lodge, and as long as there are several of you to share the same room, the Bright Angel Lodge. The latter is closed from January until March: Otherwise, there are three other groups of bungalows or hotels: The Thunderbird Lodge, Kachina Lodge and El Tovar Hotel. It

131

is more than **advisable** to phone two or three days in **advance for a booking** in the height of the **season** (mid-July to mid-August); there is one phone number for all the places to stay: 638-2631. If you want to send for the prices for the year, write to Fred Harvey, Grand Canyon, AZ 86023.

There are very well equipped **camping grounds** at Grand Canyon Village (open all year) and at Desert View (open May 1-October 15). You can't stay longer than a week and it's not posssible to book.

There is quite a **choice** of ways to see the Canyon: a plane trip over it, going down into it on a **mule** or on foot, or a coach trip around the rim. In fact, it is impossible, in summer, to get a mule, unless you have booked one at least four months in advance . . . such is the success of this means of transport. The helicopter trip costs thirty-odd dollars, but you can be sure that you will never **regret** it. Only a helicopter can give you an idea of the **scale** of the place. It is as well to check the visibility before going to the **heliport**. 9:00 is usually the best time; there is still some shadow to bring out the contrasts and the sky is clearer than in the afternoon. The *Grand Canyon Helicopter Company* will come and pick you up, in a mini-bus, to take you to the heliport, which is five kms from the rim. Ask for **details** at the Tourist Center.

NARRATIVE

Bruce flies from Mexico City to Phoenix, Arizona. Bruce has been on the road for several months now, hopping from one **metropolis** to the next. It's about time now to get away from the **urban blight** and out into the country. Here in Arizona, is Bruce's rendez-vous with his friend, Gwen Wagner. They drive out of the sprawling city and into the clear and open desert. Their destination is the awe-inspiring Grand Canyon. Once at the Canyon's rim, they abandon their car for a more primitive means of transport: Bruce and Gwen will descend to the Canyon's **floor** on mules.

DIALOGUE

Bruce: Gee, Gwen, I don't know if this is such a good idea. I mean, what if my **donkey missteps** and we **topple over** the edge.

Gwen: First of all Bruce, this is a mule, not a donkey. And second of all, this is a **sure-footed** mule who's made this trip at least a thousand times before.

Bruce: But Gwen, look over the edge, the Canyon must be a mile deep ...

Gwen: Oh Bruce, stop being such a **wimp**, quit **whining** and hop up in your **saddle**.

Bruce: Okay, okay. As long as you go first.

[Bruce and Gwen **mount** their mules and proceed down the Canyon's winding trail.]

Gwen: What do you think, Bruce?

Bruce: I'm **speechless**. I've never seen anything so beautiful. Look across the Canyon, there on the opposite wall. I've never seen such vivid reds and oranges.

133

Gwen: Yes, and the colors change as the day progresses. At dawn there are soft pinks, at noon it's bright yellow, and at dusk the Canyon often gets blood red.

Bruce: So you've done this trip before?

Gwen: Yes, at least a dozen times.

Bruce: I can see why you wouldn't tire of it . . . Do you know how the Canyon was made, Gwen?

Gwen: Yes. Do you see that river way down below us?

Bruce: Yeah.

Gwen: That's the Colorado River and for millions of years it's been cutting away at the rock and digging this Canyon.

Bruce: You mean that little river made this gigantic cut in the earth?

Gwen: Well, as you'll see when we get down to it, the river isn't so little. And, of course, the canyon wasn't made overnight--it's been wearing away at the rock since the time of the **dinosaurs**.

Bruce: There must be **fossils** in this area then.

Gwen: Yes, the canyon is rich in fossils as well as Native American artifacts.

Bruce: From what I've heard, this whole area of the Southwest is rich in Indian culture.

Gwen: It is. If you were staying for a little bit longer, I would take you to some Indian ruins, as well as to some **reservations**.

Bruce: Next time I come to visit I'd certainly like to do that. You know, I've been out in this clear desert air for only a couple of days, but I **swear** I feel much healthier. I've been breathing too much smog.

Gwen: Good. Now you have a medical reason to come visit more often. Next time you're out here, we can also **go backpacking** and explore other parts of this **vast** canyon.

Bruce: I'd like that. Of all the many natural wonders I've visited--Victoria Falls, Mt. Fuji, Ayer's Rock, The Swiss Alps--this is the most spectacular.

DISCUSS

1. What's your favorite natural wonder? Why? What are those you have visited and which would you like to see?

2. More of the earth's population than ever before lives in cities. But everyone likes to get out to the country and explore nature once in a while.   What are popular outdoor activities in your country?

3. Bruce suffers from **acrophobia**. Describe some of what people feel in situations of high altitude. What are some other fears people suffer from? What careers or situations would cause these people anxiety?

4. There are disputes in many areas of the United States, Canada and South America about land rights between Native Americans and the respective governments over ownership of land. Many of the **treaties** signed by the Indians and the United States Government were later broken. Many mining, hunting and cultivation agreements are still being disputed in Brazil, Ecuador, Central America and the United States. Who should have the land that was once originally Indian? Should people be compensated by the government? What territorial disputes between countries are you familiar with? What happened to the people in these cases?

5. A clean, efficient method for producing electricity is **hydropower**. Producing electricity in this manner, however, often involves building dams that will flood beautiful and **pristine** canyons, like the Grand Canyon. Is hydropower a good idea in cases where wilderness is spoiled? What are its advantages and disadvantages? How can the industrial and energy needs of modern society be balanced against preserving the environment?

WRITE

You are granted a one-week vacation to escape the city as a prize for having gotten a hole-in-one in a golf tournament.   In an essay of about 125 words, plan a trip to some natural wonder to which you've never been.   Explain why you want to go there.   What would you take there?   Where will you sleep?   How will you get about?

ACTIVE VOCABULARY REVIEW

The words are in alphabetical order. The definitions are scrambled in each group. AS A GLOSSARY to understand the lesson, find the word alphabetically and select the definition that fits the context. AS AN EXERCISE, write the correct word next to each definition. To save time, you can do the exercise orally in class and then write it as homework.

acrophobia:_____ totally, completely

absolutely:_____ reservation

accommodation:_____ a good idea

advance booking:_____ abnormal fear of heights

advisable:_____ lodging, a place to stay

to astound: _____ selection

bungalow:_____ prepared for business

camping grounds:_____ a small house

choice:_____ to amaze

commercialized:_____ area for sleeping outdoors

to deserve:_____ a large prehistoric animal

details:_____ to be worthy of

dinosaur: _____ particular information, specifics

disappointed:_____ represent something fairly

to do something justice:_____ not satisfied

donkey: _____ creature remains of a past geological age

fantastic:_____ animal like a small horse with long ears

floor: _____ wonderful, unbelievable

fossil:_____ to carry provisions on one's back

to go backpacking:_____ the bottom surface

heliport:_____ electrical power produced by water

hydropower:_____ a large city

metropolis:_____ to make a wrong step

to misstep:_____ to climb up on something

to mount: _____ a landing pad or field for helicopters

mule: _____ maintained

preserved: _____ a general opinion of something or someone

pristine: _____ to feel sad about something

to regret: _____ pure, unspoiled

reputation: _____ a cross between a donkey and a horse

reservation: _____ the remains of ancient buildings

rim: _____ the seat for a horse rider

ruins: _____ content, happy

saddle: _____ land set aside for Native American Indians

satisfied: _____ the border or edge

scale: _____ view

scenery: _____ people established in a new place

season: _____ smallest

settlers: _____ size

slightest: _____ time of year: spring, summer, fall, winter

speechless: _____ a formal pact or agreement

sure-footed: _____ to fall over

to swear: _____ steady, stable

to topple over: _____ unable to speak

treaty: _____ to assert with conviction

unique: _____ run-down area of a city

urban blight: _____ the only one, special

vast: _____ a weak person without courage

to whine: _____ very large in size

wimp: _____ to complain

Gwen: So, Bruce, you've been to quite a few natural wonders. Is the Grand Canyon really the most impressive one you've seen?

Bruce: Well, I was definitely feeling some very strong emotions as we sat on the edge of that gigantic canyon. It was probably fear.

Gwen: Yes, I know. You were speechless there for awhile.

Bruce: As an American, I can't help but be proud of our American natural wonders, and that famous Canadian one too, Niagara Falls. We're Americans and they're Canadians, but we share the Falls, right?

Gwen: I guess, but I know some Canadians who would say that they're Canada's Falls.

Bruce: Well it doesn't all belong to them, but the Canadian side certainly is more impressive.

Gwen: So Niagara Falls is your favorite natural wonder.

Bruce: No, in fact my favorite natural wonder is that amazing rock in the middle of the Australian Outback: Ayer's Rock. I drove out into the desert to see it, and I was really struck by its sheer size and color. What's your favorite natural wonder?

Gwen: I haven't seen many, but the Swiss Alps are the most beautiful mountains I've ever seen. I was on a backpacking trip led by two Swiss and the sights of the countryside were just incredible. Of course, the Swiss are reputed to be excellent hikers and backpackers. So we were probably taken to the best spots.

Bruce: Quite likely. Aside from natural wonders, I love to be outdoors enjoying natural scenery, spectacular or not. When I traveled to Ireland I couldn't get enough of being outside. I went camping with an Irishman--a friend I'd made in London and we had a great time. I'll never forget those green Irish hills. . . and there's nothing like the Irish sense of hospitality.

Gwen: Right, I know what you mean about natural scenery. My favorite country for landscape is Spain. Some parts of Spain are like a desert. Everything is dry and brown and you wonder how the Spaniards manage to grow anything from rock.

Bruce: Oh, but they do. I've had Spanish oranges, and they're my favorites.

NATIONALITY WORDS

As *an American,* I can't help but be proud of our *American* natural wonders.
We're *Americans* and they're *Canadians . . .*
. . . they're *Canada's* Falls.
The *Canadian* side is certainly more impressive.
I was on a back-packing trip led by two *Swiss.*
I went camping with *an Irishman.*
I'll never forget those green *Irish* hills.
. . . you wonder how *the Spaniards* manage to grow anything from rock.

REVIEW

Words concerning nationality fall into two categories: nouns and adjectives. There is only one adjective form but there are several noun forms for: country, language, people (singular and plural or collective).

e.g.   There are several *Irish* restaurants and pubs in Alexandria, Virginia. (adjective)

Many Americans tour *Ireland* every year. (country)

Irish is spoken by very few *Irishmen* today. (language; people, singular)

The Irish have a great number of narrative songs. (people, collective)

VOCABULARY VARIATIONS

I couldn't get enough of being outside.
I really enjoyed being outside.
I wanted to be outside all the time.

Quite likely . . .
Most likely . . .
You're probably right.

They're Canada's Falls.
The Falls belong to Canada.

There's nothing like the Irish sense of hospitality.
No one can match the Irish sense of hospitality.
There's no comparison of the Irish sense of hospitality.

PRACTICE

A. Which of the following pairs of sentences is correct? Write a <u>C</u> next to the correct one.

1.   _____ Japanese are famous for being very respectful to their elders.

        _____ The Japanese are famous for being respectful to their elders.

2.   _____ Carol lives in France; her husband is a French.

        _____ Carol lives in France; her husband is a Frenchman.

3. _____ I'm not very fond of Americans' literature.
   _____ I'm not very fond of American literature.

4. _____ The Spaniard are very proud of their culture.
   _____ The Spaniards are very proud of their culture.

5. _____ China food is my favorite.
   _____ Chinese food is my favorite.

6. _____ Swiss are well-known for the delicious chocolate they export.
   _____ The Swiss are well-known for the delicious chocolate they export.

7. _____ The French is spoken in Switzerland, too.
   _____ French is spoken in Switzerland, too.

8. _____ The Dane invaded both England and Ireland.
   _____ The Danes invaded both England and Ireland.

9. _____ Australian lamb is exported to the U.S.A.
   _____ Australia lamb is exported to the U.S.A.

10. _____ English is widely spoken in the world.
    _____ The English is widely spoken in the world.

B. Write the following sentences in another way, making use of the adjective or noun form of the words in *Italics*.

e.g.　Yesterday I bought some beautiful *shoes from Italy*.
　　　Yesterday I bought some beautiful *Italian shoes*.

1. All of the *people* I've met *from Germany* were very friendly.

2. The national soccer team *of Brazil* is quite strong.

3. It's obvious that *a woman from England* would have an English accent.

4. In my English class there were 10 *girls from Japan,* five *boys from Mexico* and two *girls from Sweden.*

141

5.   *People in America* generally learn to drive by the age of sixteen.

6.   Cars *from Japan* are exported all over the world.

7.   Many countries *from Africa* are developing local industries.

8.   The wines *from France* win many international competitions.

9.   The rivers and lakes *in Canada* are generally frozen in the winter.

10.   The people *in Spain* are preparing for the Olympic Games.

C. Identify the part of speech of the following words and then use them to form sentences of your own.

e.g.   Englishmen - plural or collective noun

        While I was in England, I met two **Englishmen**: Charles and Geoffrey.

        Or, Soccer is almost an addiction with **Englishmen**.

1.   English -

2.   Scandinavians -

3.   A Japanese -

4.   American -

5.   The French -

6.   An African -

7.   The Swedes -

8.   Danish -

9.   A German -

10.   The Brazilians -

GLOSSARY

absolutely: totally; completely

abstract art: art which represents symbols; not realities

academic: a professor in a university

accent: distinguishing manner of pronounciation

accommodation: lodging; a place to stay

to accompany: to go with

accuracy: condition of being without mistakes; exactness

Achilles' heel: a weak, vulnerable point

a couple: two; a few

acrophobia: abnormal fear of heights

adequacy: appropriateness

adrenalin: a heart-quickening hormone

advance booking: reservation

advisable: a good idea

to advocate: to speak in favor of; to recommend

affection: feelings of love

alien: creature from outer space

to allocate: to assign as a share; to distribute

altitude: height

amateur: not professional

ambulance: a vehicle equipped to transport the sick or wounded

amicable: friendly; peaceable

amusement park: park with recreational rides: roller coaster, Ferris wheel, etc.

Antarctica: continent around the South Pole

antenna: aerial for transmitting or receiving radio waves

anticipation: act of realizing in advance; expectation

annual: yearly

banquet: an elaborate meal

beeper: instrument to signal a telephone call

appropriate: proper; suitable

apt. [abbrev.]: apartment

artsy [informal]: trying to be artistic

asteroid belt: group of small planets between Mars and Jupiter

astronauts: people who explore space

atmosphere: the layer of gases around a planet

awesome: inspiring, respect and wonder

B

bachelor of arts, of science: degree, four-year college

back on track: a return to normal functioning

barbed tongue: ability to criticize

bend: place where a river turns

biting: sarcastic

to be bored out of one's mind: to be very bored

to be off: to go; to travel

benefits: insurance, etc. given by an employer

blacks: African-American people of African descent

bleak: cold, harsh and gloomy

blob: a small drop (of color)

blow [n]: a hard hit

boatswain: ship foreman; not an officer

boiler: makes steam for heat or running machinery

body of water: e.g., lake, river, ocean, sea, etc.

to bone up on [slang]: to do work on; to researc

bonus: extra pay

book-length: as long as a book

booster rocket: rocket that sends a spacecraft up into space

bronze: a sculpture made of bronze metal

bungalow: small house

brutish: savage stupid, mean

bureaucracy: government employees

burgeoning: growing

C

calligraphy: beautiful handwriting

camping grounds: area for sleeping outdoors

canvas: an oil painting (on canvas)

Cape Kennedy: place in Florida where rockets are launched into space

cardboard: hard paper material

career: profession or occupation

career change [n.]: a move from one career to another

cargo: contents of a ship

carving: a sculpture made of wood

casket: a box in which a corpse is buried

to catch [slang]: to watch, to see

charming: having an attractive, friendly personality

to chat: to talk in an easy, gossipy manner

choice: selection

clamor: a loud noise

classified: secret, for the military

class struggle: the fight between the rich and the poor

clinician: doctor who works in a clinic

clips: a journalist's articles

close call: a near accident

to clot: when blood forms into lumps

cockpit: where the pilots sit and fly the plane

Cold War: hostile relations between the U.S. and the U.S.S.R.

collection: group of items gathered from various places

collective: taken all together; total

comment: remark; observation

commercialized: prepared for business

compassion: the feeling of sympathy

to compliment: to praise, to say something is good

composition: the make-up or arrangement of a thing

concentration: emphasis

concretely: in reality; actually

condensed: a shortened version

con man: a confidence man who deceives to steal

condensed: a shortened version

conglomeration: a group

to consider: to think about in order to decide

contact lenses: small, flexible lenses put on the eyes

to convince: to persuade by argument or evidence

copy [n.]: a specimen of a book, magazine, etc.

copy: written material

copy editor: one who edits articles, etc.

to copy: to reproduce; to do the same thing

core: the heart, center

cornea: transparent outer coat protecting the eyeball

countdown: checking of the rocket before launch to the final seconds, 10, 9, 8, 7, etc.

cowboy: a horseman who works on a ranch

cramped: with little space

creative juices: inspiration a person has for creating

creative writing: e.g. fiction, poetry, etc.

criticism: analysis of merits and worth

to criticize: 1. to find fault with; 2. to judge as a critic

crying need: a desperate, strong need

cum laude: with honors

cutting-edge: most advanced

D

dairy: farm where milk, butter, etc. are produced

data bank: computer memory with stored information computer

daydream: pleasant thought; fancy

dazzling: amazing, bright and active

deadline: time for completion

deck department: ship maintenance, docking, etc.

delightful: giving pleasure; enjoyable

delta: triangular branching end of a river

Delta Queen: name of the river boat

demeaning: degrading, humbling

demoralized: discouraged, depressed

dishes: particular kinds of food

dental: related to the teeth

to deploy: to put in place; to install

diabetes: disease associated with excessive sugar in the blood

dialect: typical language of a region

dialysis: a process to purify the blood

dinosaur: a large prehistoric animal

disappointed: not satisfied

Disney World: large amusement park in Florida

disorder: abnormal function; infirmity

disparity: difference

dissertation: research report for the Ph.D. degree

details: particular information, specifics

dividend: payment from company profits

to donate: to give voluntarily

donkey: animal like a small horse with long ears

donor: person who gives something

double scotch: twice the normal amount of **whiskey**

down and out: depressed; discouraged

draft beer: beer from a barrel

drama: excitement; emotion; tension

drawing: an art piece made with pencil or pen

due: proper; rightful; suitable

dozen: twelve

E

ear: ability to imitate voices, dialects, etc.

editorial: newspaper statement with the publisher's opinion

to emanate: to come forth; to arise; to emerge

to emulate: to try to equal or surpass

to enact: to carry out in action

to engross: to take the entire attention of

epic: a long poem with heroic characters

epitaph: brief statement in memory of a dead person

espionage: spying

ethical: morally correct; fair; just

ethnic: pertaining to a specific culture and people

exodus: a mass emigration

everyday: common

extraterrestrial: not from the planet Earth

to greet: to address in welcome
guideline: a suggestion for a future course of action
guinea pigs: small animals used in scientific experiments
gutsy [slang]: brave; defiant; courageous

F

to facilitate: to make easy; to lessen the work of
fantastic: wonderful, unbelievable
fast food: food at McDonald's, Burger King, etc.
fax: machine that transmits documents
to feast: to eat delicious food abundantly
to feel as good as new: to be completely healed
felony: a very serious crime
to festoon: to decorate; to adorn
fit: sudden impulse
field: area of knowledge or work
fit: sudden impulse
floor: the bottom surface
-fold [suffix]: times as many or much: 10-fold
flying saucer: a spaceship not from Earth
for old time's sake: in memory of past experiences
floor: the bottom surface
frantic: agitated; frenetic; over excited
freelancer: a writer or artist who takes on special jobs
free verse: poetry not restricted by rules about meter, rhyme, etc.
freighter: ship with cargo, not passengers
freshman: first-year college student
to frustrate: to prevent from achieving a goal; to thwart
funeral: ceremonies for the burial of the dead
futuristic: of or pertaining to the future

H

hassle: problem, confusion
headlines: title of a newspaper article
health insurance: a plan to cover medical expenses
heartbeat: pulsation of the heart
to heighten: to increase; to intensify; to enhance
heliport: a landing pad or field for helicopters
help wanteds: classified newspaper ads listing jobs
herein: in something mentioned before
highlight: the most important or interesting part
high-pressure: stressful, difficult
high-resolution: very clear; accurate; precise
host: a great number
human race: human beings; people; mankind
hustle and bustle: busy, noisy activity
hustler: con man; one who pressures to get money
hydropower: electrical power produced by water

G

gallery: a place where art is displayed
gaping: wide difference
generalist: one who is not a specialist
geology: science of the Earth's history and composition
glasnost: Gorbachev's policy of openness in the Soviet Union
glut: excessive supply
to go up: to be built
grant: money given to create art or do research
grandfather: founder, leading figure
graphic artist: draws, designs, diagrams for commercial purposes
great-grandfather: grandfather's father

I

illiteracy: the inability to read
image: a representation of a person or thing
immigrant: person who has come to a new country
Impressionists: Monet, Picasso, Degas, Seurat, Van Gogh, etc.
income: money earned
indignity: an insult to one's dignity
inexhaustible: very abundant; tireless; infinite
infant mortality: death rate of babies before age one
informal sector: business not regulated by the government
infrastructure: water system, transportation, roads, etc.
in shape [informal]: in good physical condition
integral: important, inseparable, closely associated
to integrate: to bring together; to make into a whole
intense: strong, extremely active
intervening: coming between
interview: a meeting to answer questions
invaluable: very precious; valuable beyond measure
Irishman: Someone from Ireland

GLOSSARY

J

job hunt: to look for employment
joke: some funny thing
journalist: a newspaper writer
jurisdiction: power of administering justice

K

kangaroo court: illegal, unfair court

L

label: a sign, name-tag
landscape: painting of an outdoor view
larceny: unlawful taking of someone's property; theft
late night talk show: TV program in which guests appear
leave of absence: absent from duty with permission
level-headed: calm, rational
liability: state of being under obligation; responsibility
license: certificate indicating legal permission
lift-off: when a rocket goes up; "blast off"
ligament: tissue connecting bones and holding organs in place
lightheadedness: dizziness
liquidity: easily converted into cash
to look down on: to consider inferior
lots of: much
love [n]: affection
lunar: having to do with the moon
lyrics: the words of a song

M

magnate: a very influential person
major: area of concentration in college
malfunction: something which has broken or gone wrong
malnutition: the lack of healthy food
manned: furnished with men
manual: booklet explaining how something works
manuscript: written text before publication
Martian: imaginary creature from Mars
mass transportation system: subways and buses in cities
match: an exact counterpart

M.D.: Medical Doctor
means [sing. or pl.]: the agency, method of doing something
media [pl.]: newspapers, magazines, radio, T.V., etc.
medication: substance used to cure or heal; medicine
mergers and acquisitions: buying and combining of companies
mess: confused situation
meter: arrangement of beats in a line of poetry
metropolis: a large city
middle ear: the eardrum and the cavity with three small bones
minority: non-white groups in the U.S.
misconception: incorrect idea; misunderstanding
to monitor: to watch; observe closely
morale: feeling of well being
mood: state of mind or feeling
motto: expression telling a guiding principle
mule: a cross between a donkey and a horse
mutual fund: one in which the investors are co-owners
mural: a large painting on a wall

N

NASA: National Aeronautics and Space Administration
native [noun]: a person born in a particular place
native [adjective]: from birth
Neptune: a planet
nosy: inquisitive, curious
noteworthy: important; significant; remarkable

O

objective: impartial; realistic
observatory: place with a telescope for observing heavenly bodies
occupation: job
old [adj., slang]: valued
oppression: unjust control of people and ideas
open-minded: willing to consider new ideas
oppression: unjust control of people and ideas
optical telescope: instrument used to make distant objects appear larger
orbit: path of one heavenly body around another
organ: animal or plant part performing some function
to overcome: to obtain the mastery over; to conquer
overtime: additional hours at work

GLOSSARY

P

paddlewheel steamboat: 19th century river boat
to page: to call someone's name over loudspeakers
page layout: distribution of the parts of a page
palatial: like a palace
paint brush: used to paint pictures
to pamper: to treat with excessive kindness
paralyzed: unable to move
partisan: a strong supporter of a movement
pass: permit to pass; a free ticket
pastoral: of country life
P.A. System: public address system
peasants: rural farmers under a landowner
peers: persons of one's own status
penalty: a fine imposed because of an offense
to perceive: to feel deeply; to apprehend
to perish: to die
personnel: employees of a company
pet: an animal kept for enjoyment
Ph.D. doctorate degree, doctor of philosophy
philistine: narrow-minded person without culture
photo: photograph
photo caption: text under a photo
physician: doctor of medicine
plant: a factory
plot: the essential events in a story
poised: balanced
political cartoon: humorous drawing of a person or issue
pop art: depicts objects of popular culture
port: 1.city with a harbour for ships
   2.place for ships to load and unload cargo
portfolio: a list of an investor's securities
portrait: a picture of a person
preference: attitude of liking better
preserved: maintained
pretty: somewhat
priceless: extremely valuable
primitive: not yet refined
print: printed copy of a work of art
pristine: pure, unspoiled
probe: device to get information about something
process: action at law
professorial: like a professor
prominent: famous
proof: whatever clarifies the truth or falsehood of...
proponent: advocate; a person in favor of a thing
prosecutor: one who accuses a person for criminal offenses

prospects: chances
prospectus: statement giving the main points of a stock
publicity: process of getting public attention

Q

R

racism: discriminating because of skin color
radio telescope: a device using radio waves to observe space
ramshackle: flimsy, poorly built
rat race [informal]: a fast pace of life
recipient: one who receives something
recycled: restored; regenerated
reference: one who knows about you
to relay: to pass on a message
reputation: a general opinion of something or someone
reservation: land set aside for Native American Indians
restored: cleaned and repaired to look like new
resume: paper with your job history
rewarding: giving satisfaction
rhyme [n.]: agreement in the final sounds of words, e.g. "fat cat"
rhythm: the beat of a poem or music
rides: rides on roller coasters, bumper cars, etc.
rigor: severity; strictness; hardship
rim: the border or edge
ringside seat: seat with a good view
robot: mechanical device which performs human functions
rolling: of land, rising and falling in gentle slopes
to rot: to become spoiled, bad
rough time: difficult period
round: a drink for each person
ruins: the remains of ancient buildings
to run errands: to act as a messenger
runaway slave: a slave who has escaped from the master

S

saddle: the seat for a horse rider
satire: ridicule, sarcasm, etc. to attack evil

satisfied: content, happy

scale: size

scar: mark left by a healed wound

scenery: view

to scrap: to discard or terminate

scroll: a painting which can be rolled up

sculpture: a work of art carved or modeled from wood, stone, metal, etc.

seaman: sailor on a ship

season: time of year: spring, summer, fall, winter

Securities & Exchange Commission: agency that controls the stock market

securities: stocks, bonds

semester: one-half of the school year

sentence: decision on a punishment given by a judge

settlers: people established in a new place

sewage: waste that goes down a drain

share: a unit of the capital of a company

shield: protective device; barrier

to shoplift: to steal from a store

to sign up: to associate oneself with; to join

sill: piece of wood across the bottom of a window

slave: exposed

sleek: neat; elegant; chic

slightest: smallest

to sling: to throw; hurl; fling

slums: poor, run-down urban areas

slingshot: device used for shooting stones

smog: smoke + fog, polluted air

smudge: a dirty spot; a smear

snapshot: photograph taken in an instant

Social Security number: identification number for retirement

solar system: the sun and the planets

space shuttle: space ship with wings that flies back to the Earth

speechless: unable to speak

specialist: expert in a particular field of activity

spectacular: unusual to a striking degree

speculation: guessing in economic matters

spicy: hot-tasting

sprawling: dispersed over a large area

spy: person who gets secret information for a hostile party

squatter: one living in a place without permission

St. [abbreviation]: street

staff: employees

stand-up comedian: tells jokes in front of an audience

stanza: a group of lines in a poem

statue: sculpture of a human being or animal

stereotype: a conventional idea which is often false

still-life: painting of inanimate objects, e.g. fruit, flowers, etc.

to strike one: to appear to one

struck off [verb: to strike off]: to move independently

subject [adj.]: exposed

subjective: biased; partial; nonobjective

sublime: inspiring awe; majestic

submit: to turn in

sunset: the sun going down below the horizon

supervise: to oversee or direct

sure-footed: steady, stable

to suspend: to hold back temporarily

T

tailor: one who makes or fixes clothes

to take a break: to rest for a short time

to take a step back: to reflect upon

tale: story

tanker: ship which transports petroleum

tarmac: runway

to tear away: to force to leave with reluctance

technician: person who works with technical material

to teem: to swarm, to be many and in movement

tendon: cord that connects muscles to the bones

tenure: a permanent contract for a professor

terrestrial: having to do with the Earth

textile: a woven fabric or cloth

the bottom dropped out of the market: a sharp decline in stock value

throat: the passage from the mouth to the stomach or lungs

tingling: exciting; thrilling

tireless: does not become tired

tissue: substance forming the parts of animals and plants

to accompany: to go with

to astound: to amaze

to be transferred: to be moved to a different location

to bombard: to bomb

to brush up on: to revive an old skill

to burn out: lose interest from overwork

to careen: to lean sideways while moving

to castigate: to rebuke or scold publicly

GLOSSARY

to cheer up: to make someone happy

to come to a close: to end

to deserve: to be worthy of

to diminish: to decrease

to diminish: to decrease

to diversify: to divide your investment in various stocks

to do something justice: represent something fairly

to duplicate: to repeat, make another

to edit: to improve a written document

to embark: to get on a plane, boat, etc.

to fancy: to imagine (oneself)

to fire: to end an employee's job

tied up: connected to; occupied with

tireless: does not become tired

to fuel: to promote, to encourage, to accelerate

to get far: to advance, to make progress

to get rid of: to remove

to go backpacking: to carry provisions on one's back

to go below: to go down from the deck to the inside

to go on and on: to talk for too long

to have one's head spin: to be confused

to hire: to employ initially

to instill: to put in

to incorporate: to include, put together

to land the part: to get a role in a play

to lay off: to dismiss from work temporarily

to level criticism: to criticize

to make up: to create with one's imagination

to mess up: to interefere with

to misstep: to make a wrong step

to mock: to imitate in fun or derision

to mount: to climb up on something

to overhear: to hear the conversation of others

to pan out [informal]: to result

to ply: to sail back and forth

to poke fun: to ridicule lightly

to pound the pavement: to walk to places to find a job

to proofread: to check for mistakes

top secret: maximum secrecy

to quit: to stop and leave

to ravage: to violently destroy

to ravage: to violently destroy

to reel: to move in a confused manner

to regret: to feel sad about something

to satirize: to attack with satire

to slump: to decline temporarily

to snake: to move like a snake; to twist, to wind

to soothe: a person owned by another person

to swear: to assert with conviction

to tackle: to attack; to deal with vigorously

to take the money and run: to complete a deal quickly and leave

to tease: to make fun of playfully

to topple over: to fall over

to transplant: to move an organ from one person to another

treaty: a formal pact or agreement

trial: process to determine guilt or innocence

tutor: a teacher who teaches one student

to tweak: to give a twisting pinch

tycoon: a powerful industrialist

U

UFO: Unidentified Flying Object

undergraduate: student studying for the bachelor's degree

to undertake: to take a task upon oneself

undertaking: task; job

unemployment rate: percent of people without work

uniform [adj.]: the same everywhere

unique: the only one, special

unoccupied: vacant; idle

unsound: unstable; not safe

to uplift: to raise to a higher level

urban blight: run-down area of a city

Utopia: a perfect society without problems

V

vast: large; immense; very large in size

vein: blood vessel carrying blood to the heart

verse: a line in poetry

vitality: vigor, being full of life and energy

vital signs: pulse, respiration, and temperature

vocation: feeling that one is called to a career

to volunteer: to work without pay; to offer willingly

to whine: to complain

to wind: to move in a crooked way

149

GLOSSARY

W

watercolor: painting done with water-based paint

water tap: faucet; water outlet

well-received: favorably reviewed

to whine: to complain

to wind: to move in a crooked way

writer's block: being unable to write for a period of time

Y

yield: quantity of things produced